DESIRE
DISCIPLINE &
DETERMINATION

Lessons From
Bold Thought Leaders

To

From

I wish for you a life of wealth, health, and happiness; a life in which you give to yourself the gift of patience, the virtue of reason, the value of knowledge, and the influence of faith in your own ability to dream about and to achieve worthy rewards.

– Jim Rohn

Published by
Lessons From Network
www.LessonsFromNetwork.com

Distributed by
Lessons From Network
P.O. Box 93927
Southlake, TX 76092 817-379-2300
www.LessonsFromNetwork.com/books

ISBN-13: 9780998312514

Printed in the United States of America.

Additional Resources

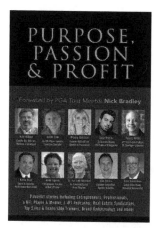

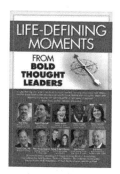

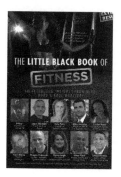

Order in Quantity and SAVE
Mix and Match
Order online KyleWilson.com/Books

Praise For *Desire, Discipline & Determination, Lessons From Bold Thought Leaders*

Everyone has a desire. But want isn't enough. You need a plan and to stick to it. Rainmaker Kyle Wilson assembled diverse and talented world changers in Desire, Discipline & Determination. *It will challenge you, empower you, and resurrect the dreams dormant in your heart.*
– Keith Elias, Former NFL Player, Speaker, Director of NFL Player Engagement

Desire is the starting point of all success. But without determination and discipline, your goals will fall short. In the new book Desire, Discipline & Determination, Lessons From Bold Thought Leaders, *my long-time friend Kyle Wilson and his fellow contributors created a powerful book that will inspire and encourage you to identify and achieve your dreams.*
– Brian Tracy, Author, Speaker, Consultant

If you want to help someone reach their potential, feed them hope. Give them inspiration they need to claim their path and create success on their terms. These stories will transform lives from every page.
– Kathi C. Laughman, Author, Speaker, Strategist

My friend Kyle Wilson and his fellow contributors share powerful, heartfelt stories and lessons in Desire, Discipline & Determination, Lessons From Bold Thought Leaders. *You will be both inspired and challenged. Enjoy!*
– Morgan Mason, Film Producer, Investor, Entrepreneur

While many assume the bridge to success is built with talent, intelligence, birthright, or luck, the successful know it's built in struggles, setbacks, and failures. Full of proven methods for real success from world-changing thought leaders, every page will move you closer to your dreams.
– Jennifer Moran, Health & Home Business Expert, Author, Trainer, Entrepreneur

If you're ready to achieve new levels of success and happiness then read, absorb, and use the strategies in this brilliant book by my friend Kyle Wilson and his amazing contributors. The lessons in this book can change your life!
– James Malinchak, Featured on ABC's Hit TV Show *Secret Millionaire*, Bestselling Author, *Millionaire Success Secrets*

Everyone has desires, but very few have the determination to start and fewer have the discipline to follow through. The authors of Desire, Discipline & Determination *encourage you to dig deep to find your desire and show you that having grit to achieve your dreams will pay off!*
– Mark & Tamiel Kenney, Multifamily Investing & Coaching

These three lessons are the most important lessons anyone needs in order to survive in today's environment. For the few that learn them, success will follow. I wish I would have learned these lessons at an earlier age. How awesome that my good friend, Kyle Wilson, is sharing them.
– Ken McElroy, Entrepreneur, Real Estate Expert, Author

In Desire, Discipline & Determination, *my friend Kyle Wilson and his fellow contributors share strategies and ideas that have helped entrepreneurs create massive success. These stories will IGNITE your entrepreneurial spirit and help set your dreams ON FIRE.*
– John Lee Dumas, Podcaster, Author, Entrepreneur EOFire.com

Desire, discipline, and determination, without these, there is no success. I highly recommend you dig deep into the chapters of this book to have your 3D vision of success enhanced.
– Chris Widener, Author of *The Art of Influence*

Desire, Discipline & Determination *delivers raw, relatable stories of real challenges to triumphs. You will be inspired and encouraged by Kyle Wilson and his fellow authors as they share their heartbreaks, personal challenges, and ultimate victories.*
– Lynn Bodnar, Author, Alignment Partner and Intentional Mom

Desire, discipline, and determination: all three are necessary in becoming a successful entrepreneur, business owner, or contributor in today's society. There are great lessons in this book we can all learn from. These real life stories will inspire you!
– Dave Zook, Entrepreneur, Business Owner, Wealth and Tax Strategist

We all dream, but these super achievers found the desire, discipline, and determination to bring the dream to life. These authors dared greatly, did what mattered, and made an impact. Through each story, you will see what it takes to become a bold leader and enjoy fulfillment.
– Kelli Calabrese, Bestselling Author *Mom & Dadpreneurs*, 34-Year Wellness Coach

Desire, discipline, and determination, capture these traits and your dreams will all come true. This riveting book contains heartwarming stories of everyday people who mastered the 3 D's and changed the world.
– Gary Pinkerton, Wealth Strategist, Proud Veteran, Father, Author & Speaker

As children, we were frequently lied to. We were told we could be and do anything. The truth is, you CAN be and do anything you want through desire, discipline, and determination! This book is filled with spectacular true stories that will fill you with hope, gratitude, and inspiration!
– Tammy Thrasher Mitchell, Speaker, Investor, Entrepreneur

If I had a dollar for every new idea I had, I'd never have to work again! Ideas are cheap. Execution is what matters. Kyle Wilson knows how to coach people to funnel their desires into discipline. He's done it again, pulling together thought leaders who have successfully created huge results and sharing their insights in a valuable book.
– Seth Mosley, 2x Grammy Winner, Billboard #1 Music Producer & Songwriter

DISCLAIMER

The information in this book is not meant to replace the advice of a certified professional. Please consult a licensed advisor in matters relating to your personal and professional well-being including your mental, emotional and physical health, finances, business, legal matters, family planning, education, and spiritual practices. The views and opinions expressed throughout this book are those of the authors and do not necessarily reflect the views or opinions of all the authors or position of any other agency, organization, employer, publisher, or company.

Since we are critically-thinking human beings, the views of each of the authors are always subject to change or revision at any time. Please do not hold them or the publisher to them in perpetuity. Any references to past performance may not be indicative of future results. No warranties or guarantees are expressed or implied by the publisher's choice to include any of the content in this volume.

If you choose to attempt any of the methods mentioned in this book, the authors and publisher advise you to take full responsibility for your safety and know your limits. The authors and publisher are not liable for any damages or negative consequences from any treatment, action, application, or preparation to any person reading or following the information in this book.

This book is a personal collaboration between a number of authors and their experiences, beliefs, opinions, and advice. The authors and publisher make no representations as to accuracy, completeness, correctness, suitability, or validity of any information in the book, and neither the publisher nor the individual authors shall be liable for any physical, psychological, emotional, financial, or commercial damages, including, but not limited to, special, incidental, consequential, or other damages to the readers of this book.

Introduction

For the past 25 years, I've made my living as a seminar promoter, agent, publisher, and marketer, working with some of the best, including my 18-year business partner, Jim Rohn, and so many others including Brian Tracy, Darren Hardy, Les Brown, Zig Ziglar.

I love learning from and being around really smart and talented people. But as much as I love and admire talent and genius when I witness it, I'm crystal clear that neither will take you to true success independent of the 3 D's that are the title of this book: *Desire, Discipline & Determination.*

In this book, my fellow authors share their stories of how the 3 D's helped them make it through some of life's biggest challenges.

Ellen Cooperperson shares how, against seemingly all odds, she questioned the prevailing experts in the medical community which told her that her son had zero chance of surviving his diagnosis. Through desire, discipline and determination, she found a doctor who said if they believed and were willing to do whatever it took, he would take that journey with her and her son.

Matthew Weiss was so moved by an untold story of heroism from 9/11 that he took on a six year project to film the *Man In Red Bandana*, an award-winning documentary about Welles Remy Crowther and how this hero, at the expense of his own life, saved so many others on that dark day.

Leonard Wheeler, eight-year veteran in the NFL, shares how the 3 D's have helped in his career and brought him to mentor former NFL players in their careers and in finding a life of significance.

7x Emmy-Winning Broadcaster Newy Scruggs shares about the power of the 3 D's in sports, both for individuals and teams, when attempting to accomplish anything great!

And there are so many other amazing stories in this book that will not only inspire you, but will also lead and mentor you in your journey.

WARNING! These stories are authentic! In many cases, very raw! In many cases, sharing the "rest of the story" that has not been on public display. That is certainly the case for me as I share my story and parts of the journey that only a few people really know about.

It's a true honor, both as an author and the publisher, for me to be part of this amazing group of authors sharing their stories.

Read, enjoy, be inspired, and take action!

   Kyle Wilson, Founder Jim Rohn International, YourSuccessStore, Lessons From Network and KyleWilson.com

Dedication

To all the mentors and influences that have shaped the lives of each of our authors. To our families and loved ones who fan our flames and inspire us. To all those that read this book and are inspired to take action, persist, and believe in their own ability to achieve great things.

Acknowledgments

To Takara Sights, our editor and project manager extraordinaire, for your endless hours of work and passion in this book! Despite the complexities involved with a project like this, you keep the process a pleasure and always provide first-class results. A thousand praises! You are a rockstar! Millennials rule.

To Brian Tracy, John Lee Dumas, Morgan Mason, Ken McElroy, Seth Mosley, Keith Elias, and all the amazing mentors and world-class thought leaders who took the time to read this manuscript and give us their endorsements.

Foreword

by Colonel Tim Cole

*"Discipline is the foundation upon which all success is built.
Lack of discipline inevitably leads to failure."*

– Jim Rohn

How fortunate I was to experience the valid truth behind Jim Rohn's wisdom in my teenage years. I learned that I could achieve any goal when I pursued it with the determination to persevere through challenges without hesitation, a heartfelt desire to be part of something meaningful, and the power of discipline—the daily habits that support desired outcomes.

That is how a small, moderately-talented high school football athlete like myself transformed playing offensive line into a college football scholarship and the first college degree in my family. It is how this 25-year old Marine Corps Boot Camp Recruit "Private" eventually rose through the ranks to become a "Mustang" Marine Corps Officer, achieving the rank of Colonel, honorably serving our nation's military over 32 years during times of both war and peace. That is how I now am able to use the knowledge I gained in my decades of service to honor Veterans by sharing their stories in rich historical context through in-depth, from-the-heart, private ceremonies.

In July 2015, I was honored to meet Kyle Wilson, Jim Rohn's 18-year business partner and the marketing genius behind Jim's world-wide following and recognition. A dear family friend with significant business success invited me to join him at Kyle Wilson's Inner Circle Mastermind. Wow! Kyle's Inner Circle was an immediate game-changer for me, and it continues to be a source of life-changing growth from a powerful group of innovators and world-changers. Since that initial Mastermind, Kyle Wilson has become my personal mentor and now is a dear, valued family friend. Kyle is a genuine connector of extraordinary people who share a passion for life and desire to have an impact on those around them. His connections and collaboration help ideas take root and grow into thriving, expanding enterprise outcomes.

This book, *Desire, Discipline & Determination*, is a collection of unique and outstanding individuals who have actually changed their world. They have chosen to share their personal challenges and life lessons to help you and other readers change your lives as well. I'm very fortunate to count a number of valued friends and colleagues among this inspirational book's list of authors and am inspired by their stories, some being told for the first time. These stories have become near and dear to my heart and if you want to accomplish your life's purpose and live with passion as I do, they will be transformational for you as well.

31-year "Mustang" Marine Corps Colonel Tim Cole honors military veterans via their loved ones. He expertly guides family and friends of beloved veterans (living or deceased) through a process of research, evaluation, historical context, and recognition, honoring their veteran's military service. Families share the impactful legacy such recognition generates along with honor and healing.

tim@coloneltimcole.com www.coloneltimcole.com

Table of Contents

"When you know what you want and you want it badly enough you will find a way to get it."

– Jim Rohn

CHAPTER 1

Not Your Typical Path, Detailing Cars to Founder of Jim Rohn Int

by Kyle Wilson

Have you ever wanted something so badly that you were willing to put yourself out there and break through any and all barriers?

That was me at age 28.

People often ask how I was able to work with the great Jim Rohn, launch Jim Rohn International, and call Jim my 18-year friend, mentor, and business partner. It was through a whole series of events, but at the core of each one was a combination of desire, discipline, and determination.

I was born and raised in a small town of 13,000 people, Vernon, Texas. I wasn't a great student and found myself getting in trouble a lot (that's for another story).

After graduating high school, I opted out of college. It really never occurred to me that I should go. I'd had a series of jobs going back to 8th grade. I was a hard worker and I had ambition. I liked making money and having independence.

At age 19, I decided to start my own business, a car detailing shop. In high school, I worked at the Ford dealership for a year and half washing and detailing cars, so I did have experience. Eventually, a local owner of multiple gas service stations in town offered to have me bring my detail job to one of his stations as long as I would lease and run the station as well. Within a year, the business took off. And then one of the best locations in town offered to have me come and lease their station on the highway. Within another year, we had grown pretty big. I added multiple additional revenue-generating services, got the local school bus contract, and we were open 24/7.

So, there I was, at age 23 with 10 employees, doing something I really didn't enjoy much, other than the excitement of growing a business and the fulfillment of providing great customer service. The hours were long. The work was strenuous. Plus I also had employees, bookkeeping and

15

employment taxes. And although business was booming, I didn't seem to be keeping much of what was left over.

It never entered my mind that some of my employees might be stealing from me.

Eventually, I had to investigate. With the help of local law enforcement, I staged a bag full of money and some blue dye. After I left the station for just 10 minutes, one of my key employees found the bag and got blue dye all over him. He had been skimming money for over a year. After he was fired, the story spread, and then most of the other employees quickly found reasons they needed to quit. Evidently, he wasn't the only one skimming money.

I went from 10 employees to just 2. I was working 80 hours a week and I started seeing profits go way up.

So many hard but valuable lessons came from those early days in Vernon running my businesses.

At age 26, I moved to Dallas. I wanted something new and fresh. I first started another detail shop.

I was doing the best I knew how. But I can't say my future looked bright. I had no bigger vision.

I ended up receiving an offer for a really great job as a sales rep for a large company. I had a company car, travel, daily meals paid for, quarterly profit sharing, and ongoing raises. It seemed perfect! And it probably was, but just not for me. After a year and half, I was back on my own. I believed there was something more.

In 1989, at age 28, through a series of random but serendipitous events, I found myself at a sales seminar. The promoter of the event, Jerry Haines, asked me if I wanted to stay after to learn about how to come to work for him as a sales rep.

The job entailed cold calling companies to book myself to speak for 30 minutes at sales meetings and then selling tickets to an upcoming seminar.

There were some major challenges. I had never cold called anyone and I was not sure if I wanted to start now. And I would have to do public speaking which terrified me. Plus, I still had to learn how to sell tickets after speaking.

The dozen or so other people that Jerry had invited to stay afterwards seemed to be much more qualified than I was. They all had experience selling and speaking. None of them seemed to be nervous when we had to go around the room and introduce ourselves. I was terrified. When I left that meeting, I knew I probably had no chance of getting the job. But something rose up in me. I felt drawn to doing this.

"Opportunity always precedes personal development."

– Kyle Wilson

This new opportunity got me excited. I started reading. I started learning and rehearsing the script Jerry gave me.

The following week when we all met again, only half the candidates showed up. What I didn't realize then was Jerry would let anyone who was willing to give it a shot join the team. Evidently, the long-term survival rate wasn't very high.

At that second meeting, Jerry shared how to prospect and book companies to speak at and how to sell and collect the money for tickets.

So, I went out that week and I booked my first meeting. It was for only five people. I was still very nervous. When I got there, there were just three people. So, instead of standing, I just sat down with them and gave my 30 minute talk. When I was done, two of the three bought!

I had my second meeting the next day at a car dealership. This was a much more difficult group. I was glad I already had one talk under my belt. There, I sold 7 tickets out of 8 people! I was feeling pretty good.

At the next meeting with Jerry and the team, it was down to just Jerry, one other person, and me. And I was the only one that had booked and done a talk and sold tickets. Jerry had found his man.

I went on to sell 100 tickets for that next event. Then I got the call that would forever change my life. Jerry said he had talked to his mentor, Jim Rohn. Jerry had worked for Jim years before, alongside Tony Robbins and many others. Jerry worked out a deal so we could start promoting Jim all over the country. He would move to LA the next day, and I would run Dallas immediately.

Jerry gave me a 60-minute cassette of Jim and said, "Listen to this guy and tell me what you think." After hearing Jim, I was beyond excited. For my first Dallas event, I got 300 people promoting the event by myself.

I promoted Jim 12 times over two years in Dallas, Houston, San Antonio, and Austin.

I had become Jerry's most successful salesman around the country. But there was one big challenge. I was hardly making any money. The commission model was broken, and I had no control over fixing it.

Because I wanted to have great events and customer service, I found myself paying for things out of my own pocket, like coffee for the attendees, and refunding a ticket when someone had an emergency and couldn't attend. I was the number one guy but not making enough to get by.

I attended a Zig Ziglar and Brian Tracy seminar where another promoter was getting 2000 people in the room. And I began to ask myself *How can I do that?* Zig was much more of a known name than Jim. Plus, that promoter spent a lot of money on advertising and other things that I couldn't do since, as a sales rep, I only received a small percentage of each ticket sale.

I knew I would have to leave Jerry's company and start my own if I were to ever get past my 300-400 attendees model to 2000+ and earn a substantial living.

How do I get 2000 people in a room? I would ask myself that question 100 times a day. After hundreds of scribbled notes on a yellow pad, I finally had a plan.

It would require me to leave my current role and lose the ability to promote Jim Rohn. It would require my wife, Heidi, to leave her job, join me, and learn to do everything I was doing. It would require me to find another couple we could partner with and who could also learn the ropes. It would require moving to a new city every 2-3 months and putting on a big event. And it would require finding two big name speakers we could promote.

By combining forces with another couple, we could limit the living expenses on the road. Having four equal partners would allow us to get the bigger numbers while the core expenses of putting on the event would not change that much. The highest expense would be the speaker fees. We would all share different roles in addition to booking talks and speaking. I would book all the media and handle all the advertising trades. Another would handle the tickets and mailing. Another would confirm the talks. Another would work with the speakers, the hotel to book the room, and the AV.

I shared my brilliant idea with a good friend who was close to the situation, and he said "Great idea! Except can Heidi sell and speak, and who is this mysterious couple?" Haha! I know. It was crazy. But I had a deep faith that there was something to it.

Just a few months later, Heidi and I met this mysterious couple and they bought the plan, and so did Heidi.

Our first event was set for Atlanta in 1991, and we hired Brian Tracy and Og Mandino. We ended up with 1300 people. We made some money, but learned a lot of lessons. For our second event, Jerry agreed to let me hire Jim Rohn at a premium. So we had Jim Rohn and Og Mandino in Chicago with 1600 people.

Next was DC with 2100 people, Baltimore with 1800 people, and eventually in Sacramento with Jim Rohn and Brian Tracy we had 2600 people. All four of us were producing at a high level! We had a well-oiled machine and money was flowing.

My confidence and excitement was over the top as I watched this crazy idea turn into a reality!

When we got to our next city, Kansas City, things started shifting. The partnership was strained. Heidi was pregnant, very sick, and not able to work as much. My dad passed away and I experienced a major injury. We still managed to get 1300 people, but I felt the partnership had played out for them and us.

At the end of the Kansas City event, Jim told me that Jerry and he also had ended their partnership. He said the model was broken and there was over 400k in debt.

Once Jim made it clear that he and Jerry would no longer be working together, I felt comfortable it was okay to make Jim an offer to launch Jim Rohn International. Since Jim now had experienced two badly failed partnerships, his current one and also Adventures in Achievement about which he would say from stage that they shut down after they were 820k in the hole, I made Jim a different type of offer. I said it would be my company, and I would pay for everything (so no potential losses to him). I would pay him 75% of all speaking fees (a typical speaker's bureau arrangement) plus we would split profits on products sold at events. And I would create multiple new products and pay him a royalty. I just wanted an exclusive on all.

We shook hands and had a 10-year handshake agreement before finally getting everything signed in 2004.

One of the main things Jim Rohn teaches is to bring value. And that was the goal we each had. How to bring massive amounts of value to each other and the marketplace.

That first year I took Jim from 20 speaking dates at 4k a speech to 110 dates at 10k a speech.—and eventually 25k a speech. I created multiple new products including the *Excerpts From the Treasury of Quotes* that went on to be a viral marketing tool that moved over six million copies.

The rest is history. Jim still had his ongoing Herbalife deal, and I was able to launch Your Success Store and other businesses plus be the agent for Denis Waitley, Chris Widener, Ron White, as well as create and produce over 100 products with Jim and many others including Brian Tracy, Denis Waitley, Zig Ziglar, and many more.

It was an amazing partnership. Jim was the speaker and philosopher, while I was the marketer, agent and running the company.

I greatly credit Jerry Haines as a mentor in my life. After Jim and Jerry split, Jerry went back to doing what he did best, putting on his own events and getting a thousand people to an event to hear Jim Rohn. Jerry and I continued to work together until he retired.

In late 2007, I sold Jim Rohn International and Your Success Store to Video Plus, who also bought *SUCCESS Magazine*. I stayed on as a consultant for 18 months.

In 2008, unfortunately, Jim Rohn was diagnosed with pulmonary fibrosis.

I, with the help of the new owner of *SUCCESS* and Jim Rohn International, Stuart Johnson, along with Reed Bilbray, organized a powerful tribute video that included Jim Rohn's closest friends, colleagues, and peers sharing their appreciation and love for Jim and the impact he had in their lives. I secured interviews with everyone from John Maxwell to Denis Waitley, Brian Tracy, Zig Ziglar, and close personal friends.

It was my great honor to deliver that video to Jim a month before he passed. We sat down and watched it together. He was blown away. He was able to hear the appreciation and love from over 50 people in his life.

Jim passed in December 2009. In February 2010, *SUCCESS* put on an amazing public tribute for Jim. I was honored to speak along with Tony Robbins, Les Brown, Darren Hardy, Brian Tracy and many others. People that were there still share with me how special it was for them to attend and how much Jim Rohn had impacted them.

Desire, discipline, and determination (the 3 D's) have played a key role in strategic moments in my life. Going all the way back to Wilson's Texaco in Vernon, Texas, to having the 3 D's to say yes to Jerry and walk into the seminar business, and to then deciding to take the risk of going out on my own.

Without all these and other critical 3 D's moments, I couldn't end this story by sharing one of my most treasured possessions I have from Jim Rohn.

Jim wrote in my journal that last year of his life, "Kyle, friendship is Wealth and you make me a Rich Man. Thank you for your friendship and partnership all these years. Love and Respect!"

Jim, thank you for your friendship, mentorship, and forever changing my life. You are missed! Love and respect! Kyle

TWEETABLE

Trust the process. Always bring value in every relationship and business transaction. Work hard. Do what's right. Find what resonates with you. And be willing to go for it when you know you must!

Kyle Wilson is a strategist, marketer, and entrepreneur. Go to KyleWilson.com to download Free his 52 Lessons I Learned from Jim Rohn and Other Great Legends I Promoted! *plus other valuable resources.*

Kyle is founder of Jim Rohn International, and KyleWilson.com. He is the co-creator of Chicken Soup for the Entrepreneur's Soul. *He leads the Kyle Wilson Inner Circle Mastermind. Kyle has filled big event rooms and produced 100s of programs including titles by Jim Rohn, Brian Tracy, Zig Ziglar, Denis Waitley, and recently #1 selling books* Resilience: Turning Your Setback into a Comeback, Purpose, Passion & Profit, The One Thing That Changed Everything, *and* Life-Defining Moments From Bold Thought Leaders.

CHAPTER 2

Courage Comes in Many Forms

by Matthew J. Weiss

"*Follow me, I know the way!*"

These words were spoken by Welles Remy Crowther on September 11, 2001.

These words marked his first step in displaying *incredible* courage after the attacks that day.

These words ultimately led Welles to become a national hero.

When I first learned of Welles' heroics, I said to myself in quick succession: What an amazing story, everyone needs to hear this story, I want to share this story with *everyone*!

What struck me was Welles' incredible courage as well as the unique manner that his courage became known to the world. It was all because of a simple, ordinary, but recognizable object.

I was a traffic lawyer in New York helping motorists with their moving violations. I never imagined that hearing the words Welles spoke would impassion me to embark on a six-year transformational journey.

Welles' performed extraordinary physical acts in the towers that day. However, courage consists of more than physical acts. Courage starts with words such as those shouted by Welles that day.

My evolution likewise started with a declaration: "I'm making a movie!"

While this statement was made under much more favorable conditions, it was still difficult and weighty. I told my friends, family, coworkers, acquaintances, and even strangers. This received a variety of responses: surprise, excitement, support, disbelief, and even laughter.

You see, I uttered these words despite never reading a book on filmmaking, studying filmmaking, or even taking a class in filmmaking. And six years later *Man In Red Bandana*, a documentary about Welles, was completed. It is a true example of passion over experience.

My words represented a commitment, a public commitment. By making a public commitment, I was now truly invested in actually starting and completing this project. I had crossed the point of no return!

"Follow me, I know the way!" declared Welles.

He said this to scared, disoriented, and severely injured victims of the 9/11 disaster in the South Tower of the World Trade Center. He said this within the hellish conditions of a plane crash, one mile in the sky.

And, in saying this, he committed to courageously save others, and that's exactly what he did.

Welles was a graduate of Boston College and, on 9/11, an equities trader who worked on the 104th floor of the South Tower. He tragically died that day at the age of 24 and, for 8 months, his final moments were a mystery. Then in May 2002, *The New York Times* published an extensive article with various survivor accounts. Tower by tower, floor by floor, minute by minute accounts.

Welles' mom, Alison Crowther, who never gave up looking for information about her son, read this article and learned about two women who both reported that they were saved by a man in a red bandana. Instantly, Alison knew that they were talking about Welles. Welles always carried a red bandana.

His father, Jeff, carried a blue one, and like any admiring son, Welles wanted to be just like his dad.

Jeff gave Welles a red one so mom would know whose was whose in the wash. And, from that day forward, Welles always had a red bandana with him.

After these survivors positively ID'd Welles from photos, the Crowthers met with them and learned how he spent his last hour, his finest hour. It turns out, at least 10 people heeded Welles' words that day.

But you need more than a verbal commitment to display courage. This is only the first step.

Boldly going…pushing the envelope…getting outside one's comfort zone—regardless of what you call it, courage requires an element of risk.

There are all types of risks. For me, my commitment to making this documentary meant assuming a weighty responsibility: getting it right for Welles' family. They had been through so much and deserved the very best film that I could make. I couldn't let them down! By taking on this project, I risked doing something that I desperately hoped to avoid…disappointing the Crowthers. My reputation was also at risk because I had publicly announced that I was taking on this project.

Finally, by making the film, I risked a substantial amount of money. You see, most documentary films lose money. But this project wasn't about money. The film wasn't made to make money. There are much better ways to invest money than in a documentary film. Rather, this project was about sharing and preserving a story that would inspire thousands!

For Welles, the stakes were much, much higher. He risked, and ultimately gave, his life.

He came down from the 104th floor to the hellish 78th floor Sky Lobby. There, he put out fires, extricated people who were trapped, and guided the first group out.

He did this amidst thick smoke, death, carnage, and searing flames.

While leading this first group down, he carried a woman on his shoulder to the 61st Floor.

From there, he ran back up the 17 stories to the Sky Lobby where he led a second group down five or six floors.

He returned a third time and led even more people out.

While many ran down that day, Welles went up.

He must have known the risks, yet he *courageously* and *selflessly* proceeded. It is hard to comprehend.

However, courage is more than commitment in the face of a risk. It also requires maximum effort.

Giving maximum effort comes easily when you have passion.

When Welles' father, Jeff, shared with me about his son, I was gripped, immediately in awe, of course, over Welles' heroics in the face of danger.

But I was also in awe to learn that for *8 months*, the Crowthers had no idea how Welles spent his last hour. Then, because of a piece of fabric, the Crowthers were able to learn the details of their son's *finest* hour. A single red bandana shifted their perspective on their heart-wrenching-loss!

There is a scarcity of selflessness in the world, and I hope sharing Welles' story will encourage others to make selflessness more abundant. My dedication to getting the story right for his family, friends, and future generations, as well as getting this message across, translated into leaving no stone unturned.

Why make a film that rehashes what others have said already? My goal was to create the most detailed and comprehensive version of Welles' story. Through the years, new information, photographs, and footage were located, all of which helped advance our knowledge of what occurred.

My team and I painstakingly crafted these assets together to share Welles' story in an engaging, educational, and inspirational way. This script was given more time and more revisions than any other document that I ever drafted as a lawyer!

We were pouring over hundreds of hours of 9/11 footage, which you might rightly imagine was very difficult to watch. Yet, it was so exciting to work for six hours in a tiny editing studio to leave with a really strong 30 seconds!

I had no idea, when the journey began, that this labor of love would result in winning a grand prize at an international film festival and a theatrical release of my tribute from coast to coast.

That *was* awesome, but it was not significant.

The greatest reward was the reaction of Welles' parents after they watched the film for the first time. Now that was significant!

It was also significant when survivor Ed Nicholls thanked me for allowing him to learn the identity of the man that saved him, and when he hugged and thanked the Crowthers for raising such an extraordinary man.

Welles' efforts were profoundly more impressive than any effort to honor his memory could be. After making those three trips to the Sky Lobby, we know that he was able to get down to the ground floor lobby. He was within feet of safety. If he had so chosen, his escape would have been from the highest floor of all survivors that day. But he chose to do something else instead.

You see, his body was recovered with a group of firefighters and a Jaws of Life.

The lieutenant in charge of the group on the ground floor had just reported that they were heading up...up to the Sky Lobby. When the South Tower collapsed, instead of heading out, Welles was going with them, back up to save others. Welles was not trying to leave when the tower collapsed. He was in the process of trying to save *even more people*! Clearly, he gave maximum effort.

Metaphorically, Welles saved another life that day...mine! Because of him, I learned that I was much more than a traffic lawyer. I learned that I had the ability to make films and, in fact, I will be releasing my second one, called *Vault*, in a few months. Welles made and continues to make me a better person.

I also learned the value of being involved with projects that were bigger than me (and that can stand the test of time). Welles taught me to be a better person. Every day, I think of him and do my best to emulate his values.

Boston College remembers Welles too. He is honored in many ways including the annual Welles Crowther football game where participants don red bandanas in his honor, the naming of the eagle mascot in his honor, the Labyrinth Memorial which remembers Welles and the other Boston College graduates who were killed on 9/11, and the Red Bandana 5K run which draws over 1,000 runners.

Throughout the country, total strangers honor Welles and his red bandana in a variety of ways, including artwork, song, and even babies named after him.

People perform "red bandana" acts of all kinds.

Courage is not reserved for life-saving heroism. It is not reserved for film projects. There are an infinite number of ways that you can be courageous.

So what are *you* absolutely passionate about?

With what *words* could you announce your intent to perform a courageous act?

What *goal* could motivate you to commit, take a risk, and give maximum effort?

I hope, like me, Welles Crowther's courage inspires you to answer these questions with careful thought, and to firmly seize that opportunity and perform your red bandana act.

TWEETABLE
Publicly commit, take a risk, and give your maximum effort. This is the winning formula to display courage and achieve great things.

After 30 years of practicing law, Matthew Weiss wrote, directed, and produced the award-winning film titled Man In Red Bandana. *The film is narrated by Gwyneth Paltrow and includes an original song performed by Lyle Lovett. Matt just finished his second film,* Vault, *a feature about the 1975 heist of $30 million, the largest in US history, starring Don Johnson, Chazz Palminteri, Samira Wiley, Theo Rossi, and Burt Young.*

Matt has keynoted, emceed, and spoken at hundreds of business events. He is a member of the National Speakers Association and graduate of the Speakeasy Program. He is former president of Entrepreneurs Organization, NY chapter and has regularly appeared as a business expert on MSNBC's Your Business.

212-683-7373, Email: legacy@matthewweiss.com
LinkedIn: https://www.linkedin.com/in/matthewweiss/
Website: matthewweiss.com

CHAPTER 3

We're Still Standing, Against All Odds

by Ellen Cooperperson

"There is always a perfect way out for you when negativity says there is no way out."

– Edmond Mbiaka

P
eople traveled great distances to celebrate *the Eighth Wonder and Our Miracle*.

I was a nervous wreck, trying to make everything perfect for over 200 guests that included Western and Eastern medical professionals, business associates, religious leaders, childhood friends, immediate and extended family, and most importantly, the birthday celebrant, my son.

St. George Productions and I had worked for months for this tribute we called "This is Your Life!" and many of the guests would share their role in this unfolding drama.

"Good evening. Welcome to an evening of wonder and miracles," Sal St. George began. "Tonight, we celebrate the birthday of a young man who has been confronted by a multitude of challenges. Throughout his ordeals he displayed a courageous spirit, a spirit that has inspired those around him…. Welcome our guest of honor, Brian Cooperman!" As Brian's favorite music from the band Rush began to play and guests applauded, my memory flew back to where our story began.

I was a 26-year-old single parent, and he was a bewildered five-year-old child who had, overnight, lost his father, his dog, and his home.

There were no daycare centers in 1972, or enforced child support laws, or the ability for me to get credit, as a woman, in my own name. And there were almost no jobs that would pay me enough to support myself and a child.

I had put away just enough money for a deposit on the only rental available in my parent's Brooklyn apartment building. I had thirty days to come up with next month's rent.

My little guy was whip smart from the moment he was born. Besides being able, at age five, to run full speed backwards and forwards and hop on one foot and rub his belly, he could recite the soliloquy from Shakespeare's Macbeth: "Tomorrow, and tomorrow, and tomorrow." He would with outstretched arms project "Out, out, brief candle!" I'd roar with laughter and applaud wildly. Little did we know, his life would be so much like that candle flickering in a sea of darkness.

I earned the rent money by convincing The Hershey Company that it was time to hire their first woman manager. I was added to their team of 105 men. I'd travel almost two hours each way from home to my new Long Island office. I'd barely see my boy before I left in the morning or when I'd come back dog-tired at night.

I made it on my own through successes and failures to eventually arrive, by age 30, in a groundswell of notoriety and fame.

Convinced that words have power and that sexist language was preventing women from gaining access to non-traditional jobs, I petitioned the courts to change my name from Cooperman to Cooperperson. When the judge turned me down in a 15-page decision, my case made international news. This was before the internet. My appeal to the State Supreme Court catapulted me onto the public stage with television talk shows, media interviews, speaking engagements, guest editorials, and articles, which eventually led to my producing two nationally-distributed documentary films.

After winning the case on appeal, I founded the Women's Educational and Counseling Center, and with support from the State University of New York at Farmingdale, built a team to serve over 17,000 women seeking to return to the job market.

The applause and Sal's voice returned me to the present.

In the darkness, with only a spotlight on my son, we heard the voice of his childhood buddy, Luke.

"We were about 14 years old, and we had these Jalopy bikes that we rode all over. I have so many amazing memories with Brian. He was always our spokesperson, and he was so smooth with girls. He's a gifted speaker, has amazing people skills, and can really make you laugh."

"Do you remember when you learned Brian had a life-threatening illness?" Sal asked. The room hushed.

Suddenly, I'm back in the hospital corridor hearing the surgeon say, "The tumor was malignant. We got out as much as we could. It was the size of a softball lodged in his chest and permeating his spine. There is nothing else we can do."

It was as if a trap door had opened under my feet and almost everything I ever feared—loss, death, helplessness, going crazy—appeared all at once.

"Did you just tell me my son has cancer…and that he will die?"

"I'm sorry," he said, as he turned and walked away down the hall.

My whole world was crumbling—as if a nuclear bomb had fallen.

I had no idea what a Higher Power was then. Yet, some force pulled me back to my feet. A voice from way deep inside began to emerge. I needed to have laser focus and the courage to face this down!

The surgeon's words echoed again, "Your son will die" and with the power of absolute certainty, I answered, "No, I don't think so!"

Fate is the hand of cards we've been dealt. Choice is how we play the hand.

I had been teaching that a good leader knows what to do when they don't know what to do. It always begins with research: who you know and who they know. So, we did our homework. I started networking and went to doctor after doctor, hospital after hospital. It seemed endless and discouraging. Two gifts given to me by strangers kept me going. The first came from another cancer patient named Malachi. His message to me right before he died was that "in a pile of manure, daisies grow. Always look for the daisies." This search for meaning, for what I was supposed to be learning, would serve me many times over.

The second gift was a wall plaque at Sloan Kettering Memorial Hospital. It said, "To all things there is a season and a time to every purpose under heaven." It was the first step to my understanding what it meant to be controlled by my spirit, not my feelings. The message was don't expect overnight results. Regardless of the circumstances, I had to keep going and trust that everything would work out.

Sal's voice interrupts my thoughts: "The search for a 'specialist' began. It was a rare form of cancer and untreatable according to the doctors.

Everyone repeated that story, all except the one doctor your mother found at Sloan. Brian, who was that?"

"Dr. Helsen—he looked at my records and said, 'piece of cake.'"

I started remembering…. There we were in some spooky basement office at Sloan Kettering with a guy who looked like a mad scientist, almost bald with a little fringe of hair sticking straight up, surrounded by test tubes, weird looking jars, and stacks of medical journals. It all looked like some experiment went haywire when lightning struck the tower! Brian and I exchanged glances, wondering if this was where we were supposed to scream and start running!

It turned out that Dr. Helsen was a center of serenity. After examining the X-rays, he talked directly to Brian—explaining, reassuring, offering options. I watched my son get bigger and older before my eyes.

"I scrubbed up for what turned out to be a 16-hour operation on Brian's chest and spine," says Doctor Helsen, now on stage to my son's delight.

Sal continued, "And you treated Brian for two years after that original operation. I understand you made medical history with your treatment of him."

"Brian was the first to have a bone marrow transplant with his own bone marrow. He was in isolation for 31 days."

I recalled that one of his favorite distractions was to watch people stop at the hot dog vendor outside his window. He swore to himself that he would someday walk out of that hospital cured and, first thing, get a hot dog from that vendor.

"Dr. Helsen," Sal said, "after numerous treatments and experimental drugs, you finally pronounced Brian was indeed cured. He also got that hot dog! You claimed Brian's success was the result of two things. Half the cure was Western medicine. What was the other?"

Dr. Helsen responded, "The other half was something miraculous about Brian and his mother. Whatever they were doing, they should keep on doing it!"

My mind wandered again. 11 years later, Brian had a very successful career with *Newsday*. I had made the pivotal shift to having my own successful business in corporate leadership development and coaching. I had also become a full-blown workaholic.

I got the call suddenly at a business meeting. Brian was being admitted to the hospital with the type of pneumonia that only AIDS patients would get.

After his diagnosis, it was discovered that the blood transfusions that had cured his cancer had given him HIV. At the time, nothing could save the lives of people with this diagnosis. AIDS was a death sentence. Again, I was told to prepare myself, my son would die. I joined a parent's group for support. In one year, 18 of their children died. It's ridiculous how hard life can be.

Again, my response to his death sentence was, "No, I don't think so!" Again, through research and networking, Brian was able to be treated by the best infectious disease doctor on Long Island at North Shore University Hospital.

Now, to our delight, here was Dr. Kaplan at our celebration.

"When I first met you, Brian, you were at death's door with severe salmonella and full-blown AIDS. I was at a loss and stunned by the fact that you had already survived cancer and a bone marrow transplant. I was not sure how to proceed. When I walked into the room, you wanted to know how we were going to make you better. I met your mother, and she was called Cooperperson and you Cooperman. I had never heard of such a thing, and she also said…so what will we do to get Brian better? She said she would help, and she asked if there were any promising new drugs on trial. A family had never offered to help before. I needed help. AIDS was an epidemic. We all needed help. I realized for the first time that to be successful in medicine, an alliance has to be made with the family. There were new meds, but they were impossible to get. Your mom and you said *impossible* is not a word we use. Your mom said, 'If there is a drug available, I'll get it.' You didn't doubt her word for a minute. The determination of the two of you was inspirational for me. I was tired of the word impossible, and with you both, we persevered."

My mind floats back in time. Once again, by the grace of God and connecting with generous people, I got to the chairman of Merck Sharp & Dohme, one of the largest pharmaceutical companies in the world. Their drugs produced positive results, but would not be available for two more years. I pleaded for my son's life. Within two weeks, Brian was in a compassion trial.

"You thrived on those drugs, came back to life," said Dr. Kaplan. "You always looked ahead. Your zest for life was infectious, and I threw the word *impossible* out of my vocabulary. You continued to thrive and bring joy and love into the world. You have been an inspiration, and I always talk about your courage. I have grown knowing you and your mom. You've both enriched my life as you enrich the lives of so many others."

Dr. Kaplan's words reminded me of the day right after Brian's AIDS diagnosis. A young male patient who had attempted suicide became Brian's hospital roommate. It didn't take long for this guy to get a piece of Brian's mind. Brian said, "I'm lying here, every minute trying to figure out how to save my life against all odds, and you want to take yours! How about you give me whatever problems you have and you take mine?" They talked through the darkness of the night and into the morning light. It brought tears to my eyes to see this young man healthy and seemingly happy on this special night.

"The story did not end there," Sal went on. The blood transfusions from the cancer days also gave you hepatitis. And three years after you recovered from AIDS, you were diagnosed with fungal meningitis. Two more death sentences."

We had almost gotten used to the drill: There is no medication to cure him. You have to be realistic—prepare yourself. Nope, I don't think so. God's grace. Connect with wonderful people. Get the right stuff. Get him cured. Move on with life!

"Brian," said Sal, "during your college years you met a beautiful young woman who became an integral part of your life. A round of applause for Brian's wife, Tracy Cooperman." The music "I'll Be There" by Mariah Carey played as she approached the stage.

"I was very shy when I met Brian in college. But something about him made me very comfortable. We dated and started a long-distance romance when Brian graduated before me."

"I eventually moved with Ellen's offers to help find a job and stay at her home until I found a place of my own," Tracy continued.

Her funny stories about life with Brian that night reminded me of the Valentine's Day after his AIDS diagnosis when he asked Tracy, the love of his life, to marry him right there in his hospital bed.

She said, "I've been waiting years for you to ask, but you picked a hell of a time. Just get us out of here, and I'll never leave you." She spent three weeks in a chair by his bedside as he fought for his life. He told her that marrying him might not be what's best for her. She said, "Brian, I loved you before, and I love you now. I cannot imagine my life without you in it, and if you ask me to leave again, I'll kill you *myself*." They married on July 5, 1992.

The "experts" told me, given his medical history, that I'd never have grandchildren. So, my first grandchild was born in 2003 and my second in

2004. They both have autism and neither of them can speak. I've asked God what I didn't learn the first four times we've faced life's challenges. Here are answers Brian delivered himself on that special night in 2007.

"I'd like to thank my family and very good friends for coming tonight and give a very special thanks to my mom. A few very special people spoke tonight, like Dr. Helsen. I became a man the day I met him. I was 14, but he said 'You have to make a very adult decision. If I take your case, you have to promise that you will do what I ask of you even if it gets really bad.' I learned then that just because something is hard and painful, it doesn't mean you shouldn't do it. Without this great man, we'd all be someplace else tonight.

"My life has been a roller coaster. Let's face it, I've cheated death for three decades now. It has taught me to say what's on my mind even if it ticks a few people off. I have always thought it's better to have five people that really love me than worry about being liked by another 50 who don't. I've learned that time is very precious, so I won't waste it. Tomorrow is promised to no one, so today is most important.

"People wonder how I cope with the many issues that face me daily. When something is beyond our control, it can be liberating in a way. It has allowed me to live my life the way I want to without fear or regret. It has allowed me to spend time with my best friend, my wife of 15 years. Tracy was sent to me by God, and she has made up for everything else that has happened. Having two children with autism was a hard one to swallow. But it's brought our whole family closer together, and we've devoted ourselves to helping our boys live a normal life. I thank God too for surrounding me with the wonderful friends and family that are here tonight. I love you all very much."

Clearly, I'm proud of my son, and our journey together has given me a breathtaking view of life and its important lessons. Anything is possible if you have a powerful reason and the determination to see it all the way through. Don't allow people's opinions to sway you from what your heart, gut, spirit, and instinct are telling you is right, even if you have to stand alone. Ride the wave of discomfort. Do not run away from fear, run to it, and face it down. Connect and partner with others to get it done. Ask big. Say thank you. It's not about self-confidence but about confidence in God, knowing that we will be given what we need to accomplish what we are called to do.

TWEETABLE

Regardless of the circumstances, or what the experts may tell you, anything is possible. If you have a powerful reason, the determination to see it through, and trust that it will all work out the way it is supposed to, miracles can happen.

Ellen Cooperperson, CEO/Chief Learning Officer of CPC, Inc., is a dynamic speaker whose Courageous Conversations™ courses have given thousands the ability to work collaboratively with others, maximizing employee effectiveness as well as individual, team, and corporate performance.

Give your employees the tools to effectively handle difficult and important conversations with her powerful online course "Connect-4 Effective Communication" at www.ConnectCPC.com. Contact Ellen at info@Cooperperson.com.

CHAPTER 4
The Mindset of a Champion

by Leonard Wheeler

I magine not getting paid for the hours, months, and years that you put into your job. When you play the game of football, there is no guarantee that you will *ever* get paid; in fact, there is a high risk of injury that could affect your ability to live a pain-free life.

That's what we ask from our professional athletes. Some of us play for years as amateurs without ever getting paid as a professional. We love the game, sure, but in the back of our minds we have the desire to play on the big stage, in front of a stadium full of cheering fans.

The statistics are startling: In any given year, there are 73,000 football players in the NCAA, who have already passed a major hurdle in getting that far. 16,000 are draft eligible. 253 get picked to apply for the draft into the NFL. That's a 1.6% success rate for players who likely have been playing for at least ten years. The 100th year of the NFL will fall in the year 2020; there has only been over 20,000 players to play in the NFL in 100 years of the game.

Once these few players get into the NFL, over 8,000 have played two years or less.

Through a combination of desire, determination, discipline, and a degree of grace, I beat all the odds. I played pro football for eight seasons before going out with a career-ending knee injury.

Now, I work as an executive consultant and speaker, an NFL Legends co-executive director, and a performance coach for NASCAR. In particular, I advise people about their mindset, transitions, and behavioral standards. Because, even if you've achieved one dream, like playing in the NFL, or getting your dream job on Wall Street, because of the nature of the world we live in these days, nothing lasts forever. It's very rare that you would ever get a job that lasts for your entire career. Certainly, it's impossible for a football player—our bodies can only take so much punishment before they give out (even if you're Tom Brady). Between mergers, lay-offs, and changes in management and focus, we all are compelled, either through force or desire, to transition into another career.

Some may ask, why continue to work if you've achieved a great deal and you've got enough money in the bank? Why not play golf, go to the movies, dine like a king, and travel?

Because that is not the answer to fulfillment. No matter your station in life, you need to be in the game. *Always*. Otherwise, you will stagnate, your brain and heart will shut down.

I went to Colorado Springs recently to talk to a group of pre-retirement executives from Deloitte about what's next. They were the Lebron James, Kobe Bryant, and Jimmie Johnson's at their company: the very best of the very best. They've been innovators, excelling at every stage in their career. I told them that in their transition out of Deloitte, they were going to need even more discipline, determination, and desire to succeed in their next act. When you no longer have a routine that is familiar to you with people around you who act like a well-oiled machine, you can feel at a loss.

When you leave a platform where you had a job, role, title, and card with your name on it—you need to *leverage* your platform. Clark Kent is still Superman without that cape (as my good friend Keith Elias states often). You still have superpowers. You still have meaning without your company. You still have character and integrity and all those transferable skills to build and sustain worth. You can still network and be even greater than you were before.

But how do you keep the flame lit in every area of transition? The solution is service. Learn to serve and mentor others. Champions are always giving their gifts to others. The Bible says, "You will know a person by their fruit." People need to eat from your tree that's been so fruitful for you. You need to create a heart of service that will give you the next mission, vision, and purpose, something to get excited about, something that will fill that empty space in your life that used to be filled by that job, whether it was in a corporation or in a stadium.

One of my favorite ministers and motivational speakers, Myles Munroe, once said,

> An apple tree may provide cool shade and be beautiful to look at, but until it produces apples, it has not fulfilled its ultimate purpose. Apples contain the seeds of future apple trees and, therefore, future apples.... Every person is born with a seed of greatness... We each were endowed at birth with a unique gift, something we were born to do

or become that no one else can achieve the way we can.
God's purpose is that we bear abundant fruit and release
the blessings of our gift and potential to the world.

Don't ever hoard your gifts. Imagine the legacy of people who might grow and change and learn from all that you've found out about life, business, and success over the years.

I had to relearn this when I went through a divorce a few years ago. It was terribly painful for all involved.

With the divorce, I got away from my standards of being a determined person. I allowed myself to dissolve into forms of self-pity, embarrassment, and worry over judgment from others. Divorce can steal from your self-identity.

That you hurt people because of the divorce is what truly saddens your heart. I love my daughter with everything in me, and to know that I played a role in her pain created pain within me that I truly can't describe. The people in our lives are innocent, and it's important for you to share that important detail with them. We have to ask for their forgiveness and also learn how to forgive ourselves.

My friend James Boyd said to me, "You don't look the same, Leonard."

I said, "What do you mean?" I had no idea that I looked any different. But you can't see what you can't see. Only people that love you and have been around you long enough see you.

I started owning my life in the way that it was. I had to create a new norm. I was still alive. I still had so much more to give, and yes, people were going to judge and murmur. But it's important to understand that some people are in your life for certain seasons, so it's not meant for them to stay in your life forever. I had people in my life that loved and trusted me no matter what my situation resembled. The Pittsburgh Steelers head coach said it best: "We are looking for volunteers, not hostages." It's not really up to us who remains in our lives through the seasons of joy or difficulty, but it is up to us to recognize the ones who truly have our back. I believe there is a friend that sticks closer than a brother. I had to also create a new huddle in my life, which started to include different people beyond the locker room. Thanks Lindsey, Kim, my mom, my family, and so many others for being in my huddle and having my back.

It was time to remind myself to get up and get back in the game. I'd stopped going to networking events and felt a little ashamed about attending. I was worried wondering who knew I had failed. But you can't hide from life. You have to pick yourself up, dust yourself off, and get your butt back on the scene to let people know that you are still you, that you are more determined, that you are more disciplined, and that you possess more desire to be even greater than you have ever been before.

I became a transition coach through the NFL and got certified in mental health first aid to help people having mental health issues like depression, anxiety, suicidal thoughts, or even doubts about their life's direction. When I started understanding how to serve my NFL brotherhood and their families, and when I continued on the journey of discovering my calling, I stopped with the self-pity and self-doubt because I knew I needed to focus on serving those in need. I stopped worrying about everything that I could not control and surrendered it to God. When I put my thoughts on other people, my focus and creativity got better.

Months later, my friend James saw me again, three months after the divorce was finalized. He said, "That's who I'm talking about. You're back!" It's important to understand that trials and tribulations are going to come, but you have more life to live and must continue to FIGHT and stay relevant for yourself, your family, and others. You are worth it!

As a coach, I would ask you what is your level of commitment right now to attain your goals and your mission? I want to help determine the capacity within people to achieve what they desire.

For instance, if I want to run a 4.3 in a 40-yard dash (run a 40-yard dash in 4.3 seconds), and I'm only running a 5.0, the capacity for that 4.3 time might not be within me. I can probably improve my time to a 4.6 instead, which is realistic. Then I need to figure out what disciplines I need to develop to achieve that goal. Keeping realistic goals doesn't mean you're not dreaming or thinking big. Putting in the 10,000 hours required to become proficient at anything—from software design, to athletics, to playing the piano—takes hard work, discipline, determination, and desire. You're not going to stick with putting those 10,000 hours in if you don't have the desire to even be in the game. It's hard to complain and be successful at the same time. You must choose which road you want to pursue.

Your past doesn't have to equal your present. The best is yet to come, but you have to believe it.

NASCAR driver Jimmie Johnson, winner of seven Monster Energy NASCAR cups for Hendrick Motorsports, is not satisfied with being a champion. He trains harder than any other driver I've ever seen. He'll take a 60 to 80-mile bike ride a day before a race. He told me, "I'm going to do a marathon," just because he wants to prove to himself that he can do one. He outworks people, and that's what makes him the best. He is multidisciplinary. He'll study as much as he can, and with his work ethic, extend beyond his abilities. He surrounds himself with people who won't allow him to rest on his laurels and who provide true accountability. A strong foundation is not built on straw or sand, it is built on rock.

Hendrick Motorsports hired me as a performance coach in 2018. This is what makes them top level. They know the importance of feeding excellence. They invest so that they can be more self-aware, create more customer/fan engagement, have better employee relationships, and keep everyone operating at a high level. They are not being miserly when they think about their earnings, they are coming from a place of abundance.

In a race at the Roval 500, Jimmie Johnson and Martin Truex Jr. were battling for first place. If Jimmie placed second, he would enter the playoffs. If he won, he would have a win and enter the playoffs. So either way, in first or second place, he couldn't lose. Jimmie hadn't won all year. On the last lap, he was getting ready to pass Mark Truex Jr. with 200 meters left to go. The wheel hopped, his brake locked, and he spun out. With the new rules, he had to come to a complete stop before starting again. After it was all over, I asked him why he took the chance. Why try to pass him when he was going to be in the playoffs? He said, "I went for the victory. I will always go for the win."

Run the race to win the prize.

He allowed himself to run to win, and even though he didn't win, he lived out his standards and core beliefs. You have to understand what you're willing to live with. Allowing our situations to downplay our standards takes away the importance of our standards.

It's important for you to find your place that you call home. Being a co-executive director for the NFL Legends community and being around my #NFLbrotherhood is truly a way I find home. I have friends and family in my new huddle that provide the positive energy that I enjoy being around. They push me towards excellence, and I strive to win with a new level of desire, discipline, and determination.

I will conclude by saying, do not settle for mediocrity, do not ever stop serving your #brotherhood or #sisterhood, protect your huddle, don't downplay your standards to fit in, be aware of your strengths and blind spots, and play to win.

TWEETABLE

Even if you've achieved one dream, like playing in the NFL or getting your dream job on Wall Street, nothing lasts forever. It's very rare you would get a job that lasts your entire career. We all are compelled, either through force or desire, to transition. You have what it takes to be great in more than one area of focus.

Former NFL player turned dynamic speaker on the executive coaching circuit, Leonard Wheeler has been a change agent for athletes, executives, and major corporations for 18 years. His competitive spirit, power to motivate, and infectious personality takes him all over the world to speak. As an NFL Legends co-executive director, a performance coach for NASCAR, and the president & CEO of TRILUCENT Global, Inc., Leonard has worked with a variety of elite executives, athletes, and organizations, including NBA, Capital One, MIT, Vanguard, AAA, Mastercard, AbbVie, MetLife, Deloitte, Abbott, USO, and many others. Leonard attended Troy University and played eight years in the NFL for the Cincinnati Bengals, Minnesota Vikings, and Carolina Panthers. He has a degree in business and another in communications. He is the author of Beyond the Locker Room *and is a ICF certified coach certified in Managing Millennials and The Human Element.*

IG: #LeonardWheeler7, info@LeonardWheeler.com, Twitter: @LeonardWheeler7, Website: LeonardWheeler.com, C: 704-577-7332

CHAPTER 5

Success Through Street Smarts & Hard Work

by Jay Hartley

I was 15 years old the day I held my mom's hand and reassured her as she lay in her hospital bed. She had broken her back, and as a single mom of me and my eight-year-old brother Brandon, she worked several jobs to keep up. While her main income came from her dream job in real estate management, she had several side jobs when she was starting her career and spent most evenings after her real estate day waiting tables or bartending. But with this injury, she would not be able to work to bring in the paychecks that kept us fed and the lights on.

Against her wishes and her warnings, I quit high school to get a job and help pay the bills. She had taught my brother and me from a very young age that family is everything and the value of a hard day's work. I felt it was my duty to do whatever was required to support my family. I already had income delivering newspapers in the mornings and washing dishes in a Chinese restaurant in the evenings. It wasn't easy finding another job as young as I was with no driver license, but I wasn't afraid of hard work and ended up working for one of my mom's contractors as manual labor in addition to continuing my other jobs. I had every intention of going back to school after Mom was back to work, but you know what they say about the road to hell and what it is paved with.

Her recovery was tough, but we were lucky that our grandmother was able to come and stay with us to help with Mom's recovery and rehab while I covered the bills. It was many months before she was able to start working again and even longer for her to be back up to full strength. Once she was back to receiving income, all of a sudden, I had money to blow.

So what does any hard-working teenager do? Well, I spent the next several years making one bad decision after another, trying to find that "get rich quick scheme." I fell into the wrong crowd, started using drugs, and was in trouble with the law. Mom moved us to a new city in hopes I would change my ways, but the move only made it worse. I was in a dangerous, downward spiral, and I knew it.

The night Mom left me in jail after I was arrested again for drug possession, I knew deep down, I would have to find the determination to get out of the lifestyle I was living or my life would never amount to much. I was in my early 20s at a time when no one should have trusted me when I asked Mom to bring me into what she had built up to be a successful property management portfolio inside of an existing property management company.

She worked the investment group seminar circuit and had made a lot of people a lot of money investing in single-family rental properties in the Dallas-Fort Worth market. When it came to me, Mom believed in tough love. She believed in me and always hoped I would surpass her in what she had accomplished in the business, but she would not make it easy for me.

That day I asked her for a job in her real estate portfolio, she sweetly told me she was so excited to have me aboard and proceeded to give me a list of properties. I naively thought this list would include the addresses of my new management portfolio. I was wrong. In her words, "You are only worth anything when your clients are worth everything." It's a statement I would learn to know well.

Much to my dismay, Mom didn't start me out at the desk next to her helping oversee investors' ROIs, children's college funds, and retirements. Instead, she hired me as the lawn care service provider for those investments.

Mom thought if I could learn to run a business and learn the value of profits versus loss in a space that let me familiarize myself with investment properties, I could someday be very successful at this career. I didn't like it, but was no stranger to hard work, so I followed her advice and started what I thought would be the world's best investor lawn care service business in the industry. I would specialize in move out remodels when a property was acquired in bad shape and take on Mom's needs for economical mowing services for her investors between tenants.

I never knew at the time she was killing two birds with one stone. She was keeping costs as low as possible for her investors while encouraging her son to build a business at the same time. Her recommendation was that I take a percentage of my profits to enroll in real estate classes and work on obtaining my license at night and on weekends.

After some time with my newly found business, I was starting to hit my stride. I had discovered the concepts of profit and loss, overhead, investment, and most importantly, the value of entrepreneurship. In the truck between mows, I studied, and I attended my real estate classes at night. Eventually, I expanded my business to include the inside of the rental homes. I added services for sweeping up dead bugs and dust, cleaning window sills, baseboards, and washing windows in vacant properties until the day came to take my real estate exam.

I took my test for the first time in October 2003, and I failed. The thought that I might be doing manual labor for Mom for the rest of my life crossed my mind on more than one occasion. I was scared. On the other hand, I was also trying to be positive and considering what a franchise on my landscape business would look like, when in May of 2004, I tested again and passed.

I may never have received my high school diploma, much less a college degree, but that day, I was the smartest person in the world! Mom started me out by having me show prospective tenants properties, running market analyses for clients, meeting vendors, and collecting bids, but I could not talk to owners. As she explained, these are people who expect a level of experience and knowledge, and I would have to work up to that privilege. I had started over, not mowing lawns or sweeping up bugs, but instead running numbers and scenarios for investors who I never even spoke to.

After several years of shadowing Mom and watching her passion for caring for other people's investments, it dawned on me. Property management is a thankless, hard, amazing, and fulfilling career that I had earned the right to be a part of. I was getting very good at helping others succeed at investing, and was honored to be a part of their real estate journey. The pieces started coming together. Suddenly, I had a purpose. I had a goal. It wasn't about me, it was about them! I could make a living and start my own investments while helping others with theirs.

Toward the end of 2015, I started to become restless. I still loved managing property and talking with my investors and tenants, but something was missing. I felt a calling to teach and help beginner property managers and to expand on different avenues inside of the property management field. I wanted to lead and be able to make the executive level decisions. I wanted to travel and speak about investing and property management. I was continuing to push myself and grow both personally and professionally.

I had joined the National Association of Residential Property Managers (NARPM) not long after receiving my real estate license to expand my education and network with fellow property managers. I was able to serve on the Fort Worth/Mid-Cities chapter's board of directors as president, secretary, and treasurer over the years. I attended every class and event I could squeeze in through NARPM, and I earned both my Residential Management Professional (RMP) designation and finally my Master Property Manager (MPM) designation.

I began reading every book and listening to every podcast about leadership, investments, networking, and public speaking. I found *The Real Estate Guys Radio Show* and met Robert Helms and Russell Gray. They asked to interview me on one of their podcasts on the topic of "Avoiding Property Management Syndrome." I was both honored and excited. That day helped me realize I could be more than what I was through more discipline and by surrounding myself with people who knew more than me. Through The Real Estate Guys events, I have been able to realize some of my goals of syndicating multifamily projects as well as thinking outside the box with regard to investment opportunities. I have been able to meet and discuss real estate with Mr. Robert Kiyosaki, author of *Rich Dad, Poor Dad* and Ken McElroy, someone who has heavily influenced my career after discovering he too was once a property manager.

Although there were a lot of closed doors, through persistence (and a lot of networking), I have partnered and collaborated with people I now consider friends. I have mentors that I never thought imaginable. Through the advice and guidance of my mentors, I recently reached one of my goals by becoming managing partner and chief operating officer of Frontline Property Management in early 2018.

Hope can always overcome fear of your past. Determination will invariably outweigh circumstance. Desire is always stronger than weakness. Nothing is impossible given the right mindset, a goal, and if you're lucky, a mom like mine.

TWEETABLE
In the world of property management you are only worth something when you make your clients worth everything.

Jay Hartley is co-owner and chief operations officer at Frontline Property Management in Fort Worth, Texas. He is a seasoned real estate investor and has been a licensed Texas real estate agent specializing in rental investments for nearly two decades.

Jay is an active and contributing member of the National Association of Residential Property Managers (NARPM). He is a sought-after speaker for multiple Realtor boards and advisory panels, investment training seminars, and several nationally syndicated radio programs focused on real estate investments.

www.frontlineproperty.com
Office | 817.377.3190
Direct | 817.288.5546

CHAPTER 6
Faith in a Whirlwind of Fear
by Zurama Arancibia

I turned to Leo and said, "What are we going to do now?"

He turned to me and said, "We'll be just fine. Have faith that God is taking care of us."

If I were to travel back in time and tell my five year younger self that I would quit my corporate job and its security to be a full-time entrepreneur and real estate investor, I would have said, "That is crazy."

When we first began to pursue a lease option real estate deal for an assisted living facility, I felt a sense of accomplishment that quickly turned into, "What the hell did I get myself into?" At that moment, I realized I had become a true problem solver. I was now responsible for the care and safety of residents and employees, both equally important. A business will always tell you what it needs. This was the first thing that I learned. Everything seemed like a problem. I started to understand that I needed to get my emotions in check or I was going to have a really tough time scaling and doing what needed to be done. It was now my responsibility to listen carefully and to understand what the business was asking.

I was juggling two things: my job and my business venture, and I was not doing a very good job at either. I had to decide which one I was going to take on full-time: my business venture or my secure corporate job? While people must think it was an easy decision, for me it was one of the most challenging decisions to make. I honestly felt like I was going to die without my corporate safety net. How was I going to survive?

It was summer when my skin broke out in hives. I have what doctors refer to as atopic dermatitis. My skin was the worst that it had been in years. I was being woken in the middle of the night to address payroll issues. Payroll is a subject that is best discussed with a clear and focused mind, and it's non-life-threatening. At this point, I was not getting enough sleep nor the rest that my body needed to replenish and act right. My hands were inflamed. The skin on my face had red bumps, lumps, and dark circles. I was not in a good mood. My husband would tell me that I looked horrible!

Leo said to me, "You are the only one that can make this decision. I see your potential and know what you are capable of."

With a heavy, scared, and excited heart, I turned in my two weeks resignation letter. It was the most liberating experience. I did not think I was going to feel that way—thrilled and eager to begin the next chapter of my life as a "real entrepreneur."

Now it was time to get goals accomplished!

The closer we were getting to achieving our set goal, the more intense it became. The intensity induced a level of pain that I had never experienced in my life.

Everything seemed extremely chaotic and to be working against me. It was like being inside a whirlwind with many things coming from different directions to distract or derail me.

The pursued lease option real estate deal that we had originally negotiated turned out to be something utterly unexpected.

In addition to a couple of other surprises, we discovered the price was super inflated with no justification. Yes, part of the reason this came as a shock was our mistake in being too excited to thoroughly sit down and review everything. We were too busy trying to have everything up and running and figured since we had done real estate deals before we knew what to look for. As far as the real estate itself, we were good with the pricing. But, we encountered our problem when evaluating the contents of the supposed business. The other issue was a broker's opinion, which was a misrepresentation.

We then consulted with a long-time friend with a heavy presence in the senior housing industry, and he confirmed our findings.

The deal went from good to bad to *OMG, no way!* I felt like someone had just punched me in the gut and knocked out all of the air in my lungs. I was panicked and paralyzed in fear!

For a split second, even before we had re-analyzed the full scope and details of the deal, I turned to Leo and said, "This could actually be a good thing."

Even through the panic, the uncertainty of the business, and the chaos, I never once looked back to say, "Man, I should have stayed at my job," or "If I still had my job, that would be better." I actually did surprise myself. Not for one moment did I really miss my job and its security. That is somewhat sad—it took me 18 years to realize that I wouldn't miss the job one bit.

What we had put in up to that point was literally everything that we had. Everything! I felt like a total failure.

I turned to Leo and said, "What are we going to do now?"

He said, "Have faith. God is taking care of us."

At the moment, for me, having faith was a very difficult thing to do. I was being asked to sit back and breathe. I'm a control freak. After a minor meltdown and panic attack, my brain started working again.

Logically, we knew we had to restructure the deal to have a remote chance of us completing it. It was going to be a tough conversation. We also knew we had to craft some solutions to benefit both us and the sellers.

Of course, the sellers were not happy, but we weren't going anywhere. We love what we do too much.

After our renegotiation attempt, the terms of the deal changed.

Walking away from that meeting, I felt myself coming to accept that *this is the life of an entrepreneur*. You invest or put forth so much time and money, and at some point you have to be okay with losing everything.

Entrepreneurialism is not guaranteed, but it is life-changing and satisfying.

The wonderful thing I have gained from every experience, whether it was a great or bad deal, is that I have learned from it and it is an amazing experience to attain. Life and business experiences such as this particular one are not learned in textbooks, in classrooms, or by paying a guru.

It is awful when you are in the middle of the whirlwind because you really don't know how things are going to turn out. But these icky and not so great situations are the best teachers and are tremendous growing opportunities. It is true what some have said, "You learn the most from the bad deals."

The moment I realized that I had to be okay with losing and allowing myself to fail is when everything changed.

I found the faith in God that Leo kept telling me about. I realized that I had to reach my goals for my business and myself. There was no turning back or quitting, no matter how many times I failed. It's learning and a growing process, and no one can ever take that away from me.

Even considering how much stress, chaos, and uncertainty was happening around me, my skin did not flare or break out in hives.

This time, it's on our terms.

Before finding faith and acceptance of true entrepreneurialism, I didn't understand why I let fear hold me back sometimes. I had fear of losing it all, being nothing, and being viewed as a BIG failure to my family and friends. I let fear get the best of me. Fear kept me thinking that I was not good enough to be a successful business owner or real estate investor. It kept me scared and paralyzed.

At the end of the day, I have nothing to lose but so much to gain, learn, experience, and enjoy! I also share this with my kids. I want them to go after what they truly believe in and what they want out of life. There is absolutely no reason for them to sit on the sidelines and only want, hope, and wish. Things are sometimes messy and unclear, but if you dedicate yourself and put forth a little discipline, you too will attain what you are seeking.

Today, something always needs attention. It is how I react that makes a difference. I don't go straight into panic mode. I take three seconds and breathe. I analyze all the angles that I can find and approach as needed. I have more confidence in my decisions and executions. Now, instead of asking Leo, "What are we going to do now?" I ask him, "What do you think of this approach?"

Since this experience, we have moved forward to continue with our original plan. We now know for how much a residential assisted living property should be evaluated. We are currently exploring acquisition of multiple properties within our chosen market, since our presence as assisted living operators has already been established.

Additionally, we have launched mini courses to help future assisted living facilities owners get the knowledge they need and the motivation and confidence for them to get started in Florida markets.

The hard lessons that we have learned are now being shared with others for their benefit.

We are also creating a platform where new assisted living facilities operators can interact in real time with seasoned operators about how to navigate and move forward with their daily operations while not feeling alone in the venture.

God, the Universe, always provides. Everything and anything that you need will always be there.

I've learned to increase my faith and trust God. I trust the process that He is working all great things through me and for me.

It is when you increase your faith and believe that everything is working for you and not against you that you start to see miracles and God at work around you.

I've seen God's work in my business, and it has been amazing. When things have seemed to be the most chaotic, a whirlwind, offering no view of how in the world it will work out, that is when it has happened. Things have taken a turn for more favorable conditions than those originally anticipated. If it had not been for the oversight on our behalf, we probably would have not started an assisted living operator business and would have not learned the business. If it had not been for the oversight, we would not have reached out to our friend who gave us the insight to re-negotiate the deal, and we would have overpaid. So yes, I am happy for the oversight and chaos because it allowed me to learn to see the opportunities.

I invite you to be bold, adventurous, and daring with those nudges that you feel in your heart to pursue a dream. Do not let fear paralyze you. Take action. Fear is overrated!

TWEETABLE
Bad deals make for the best lessons. Pay attention, learn those lessons, and do not get discouraged. Stay strong and move forward. You will only get stronger and smarter. #allowyourselftofail #moveforward

Zurama Arancibia is currently active in real estate investing, expanding the assisted living facility operations and building network databases of interested investors to participate in assisted living facilities in Florida.

Zurama hopes to encourage and motivate other individuals to take charge of their lives and not be afraid to try something new and wild. Zurama has a BA from the DeVry University in business administration with a concentration in project management and CORE Training as an assisted living facilities admin.

You can reach Zurama here:
www.zuramaarancibia360.com
https://www.facebook.com/zurama.leon

CHAPTER 7

You Can Do Hard Things

by Benjamin Goodwin

"We must all suffer from one of two pains: the pain of **discipline** *or the pain of* **regret**. *The difference is* **discipline** *weighs ounces while* **regret** *weighs tons."*

– Jim Rohn

"Honey, I think I am going to have to drop out...." Then, through tears, I managed to squeak out the words, "before they kick me out...I am failing!"

"Then what? Go back to the everyday grind you dislike so much?" said Eve, my spouse of 15 years, in her soft but stern voice. "You quit your job more than six months ago to pursue your passion," she said. "You CAN do hard things!"

I knew Eve was right. I had decided to apply for law school in 2015 and was accepted to a local school here in Washington. In January 2016, Eve was involved in a terrible car wreck that left her bedridden for nearly six months while she was still trying to nurse our then 18-month old son, and in June of that same year, I quit my job as a corporate trainer at a Fortune 100 company to start my new journey.

The significance of starting law school was huge for my family. I was the first person in my family to attend college and graduate with a bachelor's degree. At that time, Eve and I had one child, and she was pregnant with our second. Shortly after the birth of our second child, I decided I needed to become more involved in my community and campaigned for a seat on the city council. I was elected after months of door-knocking every weeknight after work and all day on Saturdays, putting up my "Vote for Goodwin" signs throughout the city, and making phone calls when I wasn't out knocking on doors or sleeping.

Four years, one more child, and a successful reelection campaign later, we come to that conversation between Eve and I.

In the span of one year I had gone from top of the world—acceptance to school, reelection, great career, great family—to bottom of the barrel where I had given up my career, I was caring for a severely injured spouse, and I found out I was failing out of law school.

Yes, I had made the decision to quit my job and start school. And sure, I had made the decision to try and complete the rigors of law school while fulfilling another term as a public servant. But the question that kept swirling around my mind was, "Did I make the right decision?" Eve and I prayed about each of the decisions we made, and we knew that they were right… but why then did everything seem to be so wrong?

If you are unfamiliar with the way law schools work, after the first year of school each student is ranked based on their cumulative grade point average. That ranking determines much of the student's life through the rest of law school including opportunities for scholarships, internships, clerkships, and most of all, job prospects. And in some cases, the first year ranking also determines whether the student will be on academic probation or just not allowed to return the next year. This was my situation, and I determined that it would be best to just let go. I had only been away from work for six months, and I was sure they would let me come back. How could I not have seen this coming?

I knew that I was not doing as well as I had hoped in many of my first semester classes, but how could I have not known it would be this bad? Sure, in all my classes I had one test, one chance, at the end of the semester which would determine my grade. Sure, I didn't have any feedback or practice tests. Sure, I had been out of school and academia for over six years. But I did not expect this! What was worse, I also did not expect this email.

> Dear Mr. Goodwin,
>
> **Blah, blah, blah…**Because your cumulative GPA after the fall semester is below 2.3, you have been placed on Academic Warning. **Blah, blah, blah…**A student who has been placed on academic probation and who does not achieve a cumulative GPA of 2.0 or above by the end of the following semester will be academically dismissed.
>
> ….

Just to put my situation into perspective, the top 75% of the class had a 2.786 GPA. My first semester grades put me in, roughly speaking, the bottom 12% of my class. I knew when I entered school I was going to be challenged. I knew I wasn't going to be the top in my class, but I did not expect that I was going to be that far in the bottom.

And so came Monday, January 30, 2017, the day I made that phone call. Hearing my dear wife's voice, and knowing the message I was going to relay, made that the hardest phone call of my life. I called to tell her that I was going to drop out of school and throw away all that we had worked so hard for. I had failed. I wanted to cut our losses before things got worse. It was in that moment she reminded me that I really had just two choices—I could give up or I could get to work.

After several minutes of discussion, I finished my conversation with Eve and sat outside with the brisk winter chill stinging my tear-dampened cheeks. Many thoughts crossed my mind in those short few minutes after the call.

If I quit, what do I tell my family and colleagues?

Can I recover from such a bad semester and not be dismissed?

Will I even be a good lawyer?

On and on my mind went. Good thoughts then bad thoughts, good thoughts then bad thoughts. Then it came to me, the quote that Jim Rohn had given many years ago and that I had stumbled upon.

"We must all suffer from one of two pains: the pain of **discipline** or the pain of **regret**."

I had been suffering the pain of discipline for the last six months, and it was hard, and it was tiring. But the thought of bearing the pain of regret for the rest of my life—that was overpowering. I couldn't give in, I knew I could do hard things and so did Eve.

The following two years were grueling. Long hours spent studying. Late nights completing my city council responsibilities. Short weekends trying to fulfill my family obligations. It was hard, but I made it out of the bottom 12% of my class, and *they didn't kick me out*!

Now, I am finishing up my final semester of law school and preparing to take the bar exam. My brother and I are working on a start-up consulting firm focused on leadership development as companies navigate through the process of organizational change. We are excited about the myriad opportunities to use our experiences to help companies cross the divide that separates the *what was* from the *what is* and accomplish the hard things.

As the evidence has shown, I am no genius. As the evidence has also shown, I can do hard things. You, too, can do hard things. I tell my children each and every day that they too can *do hard things*. They have seen my example that accomplishing difficult tasks is possible. There is no special formula, no secret sauce to doing hard things. You must want to, and you must be willing to be disciplined. Go out there and front load your experiences with the pain of discipline and enjoy the rewards without regret. You CAN *do hard things*.

TWEETABLE
There is no special formula, no secret sauce to doing hard things. You must be willing, and you must be disciplined. You CAN do hard things.

Benjamin Goodwin is a father of three children. He and his saint of a wife, Eve, have been married for over 17 years. Benjamin is serving his second term on the city council in Lynnwood, WA, and third year as council president elected by his council colleagues. Before attending law school, Benjamin worked as an organizational management practitioner focused on getting buy-in from executive level leaders to incorporate and facilitate change management principles at a Fortune 100 company in Issaquah, WA. Benjamin brings his humor and life stories to groups large and small, encouraging people in their ability to overcome obstacles and do hard things. To contact Benjamin for speaking or training events, email him at Benjamin.goodwin23@gmail.com.

CHAPTER 8

Trust God to Direct You to Your True Purpose

by Michael J. Flight

The complexity of Greek and Hebrew was a sign from God that I should not be a Lutheran pastor.

That was my sophomore year in college. My true calling came to me when my brother Jeff and I attended a "Get Rich in Real Estate with Nothing Down" seminar. That was around 1984. From then on I was bitten by the real estate bug.

My brother and I went out and immediately started trying to find houses to buy with no money down. We were quickly disabused since Jeff had just graduated from college with a straight commission job, and I was still in college with a part-time janitorial job. I then started taking real estate courses at the local community college while attending Concordia College full-time for my bachelor's degree. I soon talked my way into a job rehabbing apartments in a few hot neighborhoods in Chicago for one of my instructors. Things were going great my senior year. I had a girlfriend. I was cruising towards graduation. I was learning about how to add value to apartment buildings by buying right and renovating them, and I was working with my father on a plan to start fixing and flipping small apartment buildings.

Then, my father died on February 13, 1986, without warning, of a sudden heart attack. He was dancing in the arms of my mother that night and was probably dead before he hit the floor. My two brothers, Jeff and Tim, happened to both be home with me that night, so we were able to meet my mom at the hospital to get the news. My dad was 52 years old at the time of his death.

This event put a large financial strain on our family, especially my mother, since my father worked straight commission selling dental supplies. My dreams of flipping houses and buying apartments with my dad as my financial backer were also finished.

I finished my senior year of college in a daze, still trying to comprehend that my dad was not coming through our door again. As a further blow, my part-time job in college was coming to an end. My boss told me he did not have a full-time position for me after graduation. Soon after, my girlfriend left me for a guy in med school. Both my parents instilled in us an ethic of hard work, but my dad bequeathed his spirit of optimism which was on display every day of his life. I also had a small but growing sense that God had a purpose for the events in my life.

I decided to go into retail real estate brokerage because of the potential to make more money with less cold calling. With retail tenants, there is an opportunity to do multiple deals as they expand their stores in different markets throughout the country.

So, I started interviewing with large commercial real estate companies. Even though I had hands-on experience and had passed the Illinois real estate license exam, they all took a pass on hiring me. My degree was in sociology/psychology and not in business or finance.

After many interviews and rejection letters, Jim Kaplan, the owner of a small boutique retail brokerage firm did take a chance on me. I am forever grateful for his tutelage and mentorship. When hiring now, my company looks for drive, determination, and the ability to learn because of these formative experiences.

The job was straight commission, so I worked long hours during the day as a commercial real estate broker and then delivered pizza for Domino's at night to help my mom with the bills.

The hard work paid off. Through cold calling regional retailers in other parts of the country, I was able to land a discount women's clothing store looking to expand into the Chicago market. The opportunity to assist them with opening 9 to 10 stores added up to some significant commission checks. Additionally, the experience exposed me to some larger shopping center landlords which landed me a job with National Property Analysts (NPA). Hard work, plus God putting me in the right spot, has been a huge theme in my life. The Rolling Stones said it best, "You can't always get what you want. But if you try sometimes, you just might find: You get what you need."

While at NPA, I made some lifelong friends including Jeff Gwin. Jeff went on to be one of the founders of Merchant Equity Group, LLC and a business partnership with me that lasted 26 years. Things were going fantastic for me with a great salary, bonuses for leases completed, and travel. But, as I was soon to learn, real estate is a cyclical business heavily dependent upon what happens with regulations both in Washington, DC and at the local level.

The Reagan tax cuts of 1986 ushered in a long period of great prosperity. But the tax bill also changed the financial model for real estate syndication and tax shelters. It put NPA into a bit of a tailspin since they could not raise money as easily as they could in the past. Additionally, changes made to the Savings and Loan regulations in 1980 created the S&L crisis later that decade which compounded problems into a deep recession. As a result, I was laid off from NPA in 1989.

My friend Cory Andrews was also laid off from his retail leasing job around the same time. I had started the groundwork for what would become Concordia Realty. Jobs in the real estate industry were scarce, and lots of people were out looking for work; we decided it was the perfect time to start a company and position ourselves for when the economy bounced back.

Another great new beginning at this time was my marrying Maddalena; my beautiful, talented, creative, and supportive wife of 28 years. She has been a rock of stability, a fantastic cook, and my personal hair stylist. She is the embodiment of the American Dream, having immigrated to the US when she was seven years old. She can also be formidable in her determination, like when she said if our sons get my last name, she would pick the first names. We ended up with the thoroughly unique Salvatore and Massimo which have been great conversation starters.

Starting Concordia Realty was a bit of déjà vu all over again, only this time Cory got us a job delivering newspapers from 4 a.m. to 6 a.m. before starting work for the day at our company.

Through hard work and tenacity, we built Concordia Realty into a premier boutique real estate operating firm. We were privileged to be involved with all kinds of unique and profitable projects. These projects ranged from redeveloping enclosed malls to repositioning many shopping centers by demolishing obsolete buildings and replacing them with modern retail stores. The artwork we installed at some of our properties created newsworthy sensations and ended up generating notoriety in major films and television series such as *Wayne's World*, *Wanted*, and *The Sopranos*.

I was exceptionally blessed to learn the shopping center business from our client David Bermant, an industry pioneer. This has led to my eventually partnering with his son Andrew for over 29 years now. My partners, Jeff Gwin and John Mannix, had contacts with large institutional investors like hedge funds, insurance companies, and pension fund advisors. We were able to do some creative and rewarding projects. Closer to home, I formed a partnership with Jim Stillo to convert apartments and commercial loft buildings into condominium projects, and we successfully invested in distressed single-family fix and flip portfolios.

I got fat (literally) and comfortable. A victim of my own success, I got into questionable investments which soon became large time wasters and an ever-increasing money pit. These other pursuits generated losses and created a rift in my marriage which is still healing. It was also around this time that I basically forgot about God.

However, God did not forget about me. My long-time friend and mentor Steve Zoller gave me the book *Halftime* written by Bob Buford. It was just what I needed to turn a corner in my life. It was time to go from success to significance. I rediscovered that God had given me talents which were not only valuable in the business world but which could also be applied to assist ministries with their real estate and leadership needs.

Now I am assisting Chicago Hope Academy (a Christian college prep high school serving low income families on Chicago's west side), Mission of Our Lady of the Angels (a Franciscan poverty alleviation and education ministry serving Chicago's Humboldt Park neighborhood), Sunshine Gospel Ministry (Christian community development, youth programs, and entrepreneurial training courses in Chicago's Woodlawn neighborhood), and Asociatia Umanitara Libertatea De Viata (Freedom of Life Humanitarian Association of Romania, an organization that trains women who have been victims of human trafficking in Romania to start home-based internet businesses to provide for themselves and their families).

These nonprofit organizations are able to utilize my skills in business, transactions, and project management to start new ventures and redevelop under-resourced communities.

Earlier in my life, I felt "less than" for not going into full-time ministry. Now I know God has blessed me and moved me through my life to have an impact in people's lives with education, poverty alleviation, and assisting investors with growing wealth. God has placed me exactly where he wants me, and it's allowed me to develop specialized skills to assist people all over the world.

In this new season of my life, I reinvented the way we at Concordia Realty did business to take lessons learned from my wide variety of real estate experiences. There is a very real need for retail real estate investment education and mentoring programs, so I have started a blog with detailed information on shopping centers and single-tenant net-leased retail real estate property. Additionally, there is a gap in the knowledge base in the real estate education podcast world. I thank the hosts and producers who have been gracious enough to have me on their educational shows. Through these efforts, Concordia Realty has been able to start our first retail real estate mentorship program with several highly qualified and motivated individuals looking to break into the industry.

Also, having seen the wreckage created by the Wall Street casino culture through three different downturns, last year we decided to open up our shopping center investment opportunities to individual investors. My friends and family members would approach me with their consternation over random events halfway across the world affecting their retirement savings. They saw the benefits of consistent passive cash flows created by the household names in our shopping centers. They realized the tenants where they shopped, got a coffee, worked-out, or dined were signing long-term leases, paying consistent rent, and creating inflation hedged, tax advantaged returns. They were not getting those benefits in the stock market.

Looking back, I can see the different twists and turns my life has taken to get to this point, and see the hand of God at work. He is gently nudging me one way, sometimes dramatically grabbing my attention to illuminate a need for correction at other times. Through it all, He has been there to guide me. My life has worked out best when I actually listen to His directions. "For where your treasure is, there your heart will be also." Matthew 6:21.

The root word of discipline is disciple. Determining your purpose creates desire and enhances discipline. Determination develops the muscle of discipline and desire will carry you through to your purpose. Trust God, and he will direct you and equip you to your true purpose in life.

TWEETABLE

Trust God and he will direct you and equip you to your true purpose in life.

Michael J. Flight is a husband, father, son, brother, friend, philanthropist, and real estate entrepreneur who is an expert in shopping center investment, non-profit startups, and community redevelopment. Michael has been active in commercial real estate for the past 35 years and has handled more than $500 million worth of real estate transactions. Michael has been featured on many business podcasts, served on numerous non-profit boards, held elected office, and shared as a featured speaker on real estate investment, poverty alleviation, and free markets. Michael and his wife Maddalena were blessed to be part of a documentary film on religious life at Mission of Our Lady of the Angels in Chicago. More information can be found at www.michaeljflight.com and www.concordiarealty.com

Contact michael@michaeljflight.com

CHAPTER 9
Life Is Difficult Until It Isn't

by Greg Zlevor

It seemed like the right thing to do. I didn't have a job and I had just completed my biology degree, so I accepted the teaching position at a prestigious high school.

At the same time, I began a residential director role at an urban home for adolescent boys. I managed the home on the evenings and weekends, overseeing 12 boys ranging in age from 13-17.

At the time, accepting these two positions seemed like a good idea. As a recent college graduate, the residential position provided me room and board. My annual teaching salary was $14,000, so every dollar counted.

As it turns out, taking on two jobs wasn't such a great decision. The dual responsibilities buried me physically, emotionally, and mentally. I lived minute to minute.

Until I was gifted with an insight.

One day, collapsed, alone, head down on the table in the teacher's lounge, I was feeling the full force of my situation. In walked Jim, the German teacher. "Greg, you look completely overwhelmed. Are you feeling like the worst teacher in the world?"

I nodded yes.

"I can tell you straight away that the first year of teaching is not supposed to be about being good; it's all about keeping your head above water. Are you surviving?"

"Yes, I guess I am surviving, but barely." I responded. Jim said, "Then you're OKAY. I am hearing good things about you in your classroom, and I sense you have what it takes to be a great teacher."

That was in March. I had somehow survived seven months and only had two to go, but that brief conversation flipped a switch inside me. From that moment on, my entire life improved radically.

Looking back, I realize it had been my thoughts that had led me to feeling overwhelmed and filled with a debilitating anxiety. I thought I was a failure, that I was incompetent, and worst of all, that I was letting the students and the school down. In reality, I wasn't. I was doing exactly what I was capable of, and that was enough.

It came to me then that I had another option: to unlock the trap I had crawled into and set myself free. I didn't have to live buried under negative thoughts.

The key to the lock was to ask better questions of myself.

How can I survive? How do I do that well?

Maybe instead of second guessing the ways I was missing the mark, I could think about what I was gaining from the experience.

What am I learning through this challenge? How is it making me stronger, wiser, and better?

This one shift in perspective balanced my emotional experience almost immediately, and as my anxiety began to dissipate, I started building momentum. I had uncovered a new internal outlook, and consequently, even paradoxically, everything changed externally.

Better questions led me to a better perspective.

I became fully engaged, and rather than feeling like I was becoming unraveled, I was able to pull the threads of my daily life experiences together and started weaving...my lesson plans, the residential home, and my personal life. I had graduated from terror to inspiration and made the shift from paralysis to action.

By the end of that school year, I felt so encouraged that I stayed and kept teaching at the high school for three more years.

Looking back now, I can summarize this life-altering insight this way: the desire, determination, and discipline I needed didn't originate from an inner predisposition; it sprang from my choosing a new inner narrative. That inner narrative sprung from better questions, which led to healthier attention, and finally a new story about my life.

The Five "Aha!" Keys to Creating More Empowering Stories

Based on this challenging experience early on in my life, I discovered five "Aha!" keys I still use to shift my thinking from overwhelm to enthusiasm.

Key #1. I need to separate what is actually happening from how I perceive the situation. In the above instance, I was in my first year of teaching, and I was inexperienced. That is a simple fact. The question I needed to ask myself was: how did I internalize this reality? Was I experiencing the job as awful because I didn't know what I was doing, or could I view it as an opportunity to learn how to handle the challenges of being in a new job? *My experience depends entirely on how I choose to perceive it. What can I learn when I'm uncomfortable? How can this learning serve me to be a better person?*

Key #2. How I perceive the facts is totally within my control. What I focus on is up to me. Do I focus on the overwhelm or the opportunity? It's my choice. No one and nothing forces me to select one perspective over another. It is my responsibility to make the choice. It is my responsibility to ask how can this help me versus why me.

Key #3. If I commit to catching myself before my mind starts running, then I am free. Without training my mind, I get caught in a lot of mental and emotional traps. If I let my mind cut loose into a confusing forest of emotions—then I am stuck. Instead, I can stop and ask myself, "Hey, anxiety…hey, crazy thoughts…who could I be without this story? What alternate perspectives of this situation exist? Is there a healthier way for me to interpret the facts in front of me?"

Several years ago, I was walking through a field one morning on my way to work. In the distance, I noticed a raccoon caught in a live trap. The raccoon crouched in the corner of the cage appearing dazed and helpless. I felt compelled to free the animal, but I feared being bitten or attacked. What if it was rabid?

I approached the trap, opened the latch and door, and quickly jumped back in fear to avoid being bitten. Surprisingly, the raccoon didn't scurry out and away. Rather, it walked out of the cage, then around the cage, then over the cage. It looked to me like it was studying the cage.

"That's one smart raccoon! It's going to study the trap before it leaves."

It occurred to me that we would be wise to do the same with our emotions and the stories we tell ourselves: study the trap so we don't get caught again.

Key #4. Surround yourself with allies that can help you out of the trap. Sometimes we get so caught up in our stories that we can't see our way out. All we can hear is the overpowering cacophony of thoughts that crowd our mental bandwidth and diminish our power. In that case, we need a lifeline.

I was fortunate all those years ago to have had a friend who refused to sign on with me when I was caught in a story in my head. My friend was Jim the German teacher. He asked me the questions that disempowered my crippling thoughts. He gently and surgically teased away my disempowering story and helped me craft a new one. He showed me that there was a latch on the trap that could be opened to let me free…if I was willing.

Key #5. By practicing on smaller issues, we build our mental muscle so that when the large issues show up we are ready and willing to shift. Imagine you're hurrying in the car to a big event and the next stoplight is red: Does this always happen to you, are you the victim, or is this a chance to be grateful you have a vehicle with brakes that work well? Every day provides multiple opportunities to practice.

With practice, we develop the muscle of separating the facts from the story (or how we internalize the facts). Better perspectives lead to better outcomes in all areas of our life and better stories give us the strength, desire, determination, and discipline to move toward the calling of our greatness. What questions lead us to better stories and outcomes?

Where I see the Five Keys in real life:

I especially witness this challenge in professional teams and organizations. I'm a leadership expert and I regularly coach executives, managers, and new hires. Presently, I'm working with an executive who is on a "performance improvement plan." At first, he fought and resisted the plan. "This is not fair. I don't deserve this. My reports tell me I'm a great leader." Unfortunately, the team he sits on finds him pushy, overly aggressive, and too protective of his team. I regularly heard, "He is a difficult team member," from his peers and direct leader.

Now, what will he do? Will he see this "performance improvement plan" as an opportunity to grow and learn or will he rebel because it's not fair? His perspective will determine his effort and performance. An empowering perspective can readily lead to empowering results…if he is interested.

Being interested is the magic elixir.

Recently, I visited an innovation center at a large university. While there, I met several students frustrated by the lack of internships and work experiences available to undergrads, especially students on visas. As a result, they started a student run organization that initiated internships instead of waiting for them. They turned the tables and offered unique solutions to companies for reduced fees rather than wait for companies to offer limited jobs.

How can we entice companies to come to us?

As a result, they have completed multiple high-end projects, gained valuable real world experience, and earned an income through the university.

When they found out what I did, they immediately asked if I would come and teach them leadership skills and provide some internships. They raised money and paid my fee. They are interested and hungry. They have the elixir. It will make all the difference.

Life is difficult until it isn't. Start and keep practicing. Practice leads to insight and skills which in turn lead to interest and growth. The challenges never end, but if we practice enough we learn to accept and even enjoy the challenges. Saying and thinking "why me" is painful. Embracing "next" is a lot more rewarding.

Let's leave the trap of "why me" behind and grow to the world of "next."

What can I do to embrace the here and now, learn, and act wisely today?

 ## TWEETABLE
Athletes practice to increase their performance. You can practice to increase your happiness and joy in life. Life is difficult unless you practice.

Greg Zlevor is the President of Westwood International a consulting collaborative that's reimagining what it means to lead wisely in a global age. Westwood's signature, global-scale action learning programs, coaching and leadership initiatives have energized global brands like Johnson & Johnson, Kimberly-Clark, Volvo, the Singapore Police Force and General Electric. How can we help your team lead wisely? Send a note to Greg at gzlevor@westwoodintl.com or call 802.253.1933.

"I am a leadership expert. I design and customize experiences for companies, groups, and leaders who want to become more valuable in life and the workplace."

CHAPTER 10
Purpose-Driven Investing

by Jim & Nancy Richardson

Autism changes everything. Receiving this diagnosis permanently changes the dynamics of your life and the relationships you have with friends and family. Autism is so misunderstood that it often leaves families feeling isolated and desperate for answers. In the best of circumstances, being a good parent is not easy; parenting a child with autism is simply overwhelming. For us, the thought of going to a movie or a noisy venue was unnerving. Observing other children playing freely at the playground while watching our child exclude himself was heartbreaking. There were many long lonely months we felt lost.

Our story and subsequent journey of raising an autistic child is typical, and likely identical to thousands of families around the world. These are families who are one day suddenly thrust into a world for which few, if any, are prepared. Nancy's pregnancy was uneventful, and the entire family was eager to welcome and meet the newest member of the family. Our son Michael was born in January 1994 and, despite being six weeks premature, seemed to be a healthy baby and developed into the sweetest, most lovable, and happy toddler. All was well in our world until one day it wasn't.

Without warning, life as we knew it came to a screeching halt. After months of Michael's non-verbal development, inconsistent sleeping, and a mother's heightened intuition that things were not as they should be, we went searching for answers. In a time before Google, research was limited to countless hours of manual digging and a never-ending desire for answers.

After numerous consultations with our area's top specialists, Michael, at three years old, was officially diagnosed with autism spectrum disorder (ASD). Suddenly, we were overwhelmed with uncertainty, fear, and dozens of unanswered questions. What the hell is autism? How did it happen? Why did it happen? And above all else, what could we do for Michael? We felt besieged, helpless, and powerless. Seeking any specialist we could find, our world evolved into a quest for every speech, occupational, and behavioral therapy known at the time, including a fruitless regimen of supplements and specialized diets. All the while, we were contemplating what the future held.

The years immediately following the diagnosis were the hardest. We found ourselves still understanding very little about autism, but undeterred in our commitment to give our son the best life possible. Despite our relentless determination and endless worry, fear and doubt remained daily companions. Would Michael have any friends? What would his transition into adulthood resemble? Would he find joy and love? And, who will care for him when we're gone? Neurotypical children depend less on their parents as they age, which is not the case for most children with ASD. It was difficult to assess and near-impossible to prepare for the road ahead.

Over the years, our search for answers and inclusion continued. There had to be action we could take. From the "specialist" who suggested we crush salt with a mortar and pestle to infuse negative ions into the body, it was clear that the Doctor du Jour approach wasn't the answer. We also realized our school district's one-size-fits-all approach to special education wasn't giving Michael the individualized attention he needed. After significant research, we sold our house in New Jersey and moved to the Central Bucks School District in Pennsylvania—highly regarded and recognized for their leading-edge autism curriculum. Through the culmination of great teachers and therapists, the yearly tweaks to his individualized education plan (IEP), along with years of after-school tutoring and the relentless drive to get nothing but the best education for our son, Michael was able to graduate high school. Many people say "it takes a village to raise a child." We believe it takes a child with autism to raise the consciousness of the community.

Subsequently, a new revelation set in. Now that Michael had graduated from high school, where would he work, where would he live, and ultimately, what will happen to him once we're gone? Back came the panic, confusion, and a whole new set of unanswered questions. Once again, it became apparent we had to take matters into our own hands, like many families now find themselves doing.

As parents of a grown son with autism, who will inevitably outlive us and will never be able to live entirely independent, our personal mission and business vision connect in a meaningful way. As our business, Stonebridge Capital Consulting, continues to grow, we will fund and accelerate the development of safe and sustainable housing for adults with autism and other intellectual developmental disabilities. As 90% of adults with autism are unemployed or underemployed, our plan will also incorporate job opportunities for adults on the autism spectrum as well as for those with other intellectual developmental disabilities. We can no longer wait for the government or others to provide a viable and sustainable solution for our son or the thousands of other families facing this pervasive problem.

The word "autism" comes from the Greek word "autos," meaning "self." It describes a condition in which a person is removed from social interaction and becomes isolated. From the early 1900s, autism referred to a range of neuropsychological disorders, including one group of symptoms related to schizophrenia. In the 1940s, researchers began to use "autism" to describe children with emotional or social problems. Autism and schizophrenia remained linked in researchers' minds until the 1960s when doctors began to have a different understanding. Through the 1970s, treatments for autism included medications such as LSD, electric shock, and behavioral change techniques. The cornerstone of autism therapy today focuses on behavioral and language-centric techniques, with median costs around $50,000 annually.

Between 1960 and 1980, the incidence was 1 in 10,000 cases in the US. In 1988, Dustin Hoffman introduced the world to autism with his portrayal of an autistic savant in *Rain Man*. Seemingly overnight, the incidence rate skyrocketed to 1 in 500, and currently, the Centers for Disease Control (CDC) reports that autism now affects 1 in 59 children, with hundreds of families receiving an autism diagnosis every day.

Across the United States, estimated rates vary from a high of 1 in 34 in New Jersey (ironically where our son Michael was born) to a low of 1 in 77 in Arkansas. "This suggests that the new national prevalence estimate of 1 in 59 still reflects a significant understatement of autism's true prevalence among our children," says Autism Speaks Chief Science Officer Thomas Frazier. "And without more and better research, we can't know how much higher it truly is."

Autism knows no boundaries and occurs in all racial, ethnic, and socioeconomic groups, and is about five times more common in boys than girls. As a spectrum disorder, it affects each person in different ways and can range from very mild to severe, and as of today, there is no known cure. Autism is a developmental disability that significantly affects three areas: communication (both verbal & nonverbal) social interaction, and behavior.

Caring for an autistic person with intellectual developmental disabilities over their lifetime can cost up to $3.2 million. The cost of caring for Americans with autism, according to Autism Speaks, reached $268 billion in 2015 and could rise to $461 billion by 2025 in the absence of more-effective interventions and support throughout their lives. The majority of autism's costs in the U.S. are for adult services, estimated at $175 to $196 billion a year, compared to $61 to $66 billion a year for neurotypical children.

On top of these staggering costs, moving out of the family home is one of the most significant decisions for the family with a grown child on the autism spectrum. Finding safe and sustainable housing options with the appropriate caregiving supports is daunting, let alone providing an opportunity for social inclusion and independence, which adds another level of uncertainty, frustration, and complexity.

Our mission is to tackle the challenges' autistic adults and their families face by providing an environment that allows those like Michael to live as independently as possible, hold down useful jobs, be connected in their communities, and have the opportunity to live full and meaningful lives. We have witnessed the remarkable strides Michael has made and remain relentless in solving this overwhelming and complex challenge. The hardest part of having a special needs child is the struggle—the struggle for others to understand your child as well as you do, the struggle for services they will need for the rest of their lives, and the internal struggle of wondering if you've done everything humanly possible for your child. That's the struggle that never goes away.

Michael is but one of 500,000 "children" with autism aging into adulthood over the next decade, with 87% living in the family home and 35% requiring 24-hour support. What will happen when their parents are no longer there? Autism truly changes everything. We've been there and continue to face this issue with our absolute resolve and diligent commitment to helping as many families as possible. We bring to our business a tremendous passion for success and an immense desire to make a difference, all fueled by the extraordinary joy and love we have for, and receive, from this amazing young man.

TWEETABLE

Autism changes everything. As parents of a grown son with autism who will inevitably outlive us, we can no longer wait for others to provide a viable and sustainable housing solution for our son or the other families facing this pervasive problem.

Experienced investment professionals Jim and Nancy Richardson created Stonebridge Capital Consulting to provide safe and sustainable housing for adults with autism, beginning with their son Michael. This real estate advisory firm manages customized discretionary capital for sophisticated investors, private equity firms, prominent family offices, and select qualified sponsors—those looking to differentiate themselves in an increasingly crowded market. If you're interested in helping Jim and Nancy realize their mission, give them a call at 267-423-4334.

invest@stonebridgecapitalconsulting.com
https://stonebridgecapitalconsulting.com
www.linkedin.com/in/jim-stonebridgecapitalconsulting
https://www.facebook.com/stonebridgecapitalconsulting/

CHAPTER 11

Seeds to Serving

by Lin Weaver

We are all terminal. Life is short and eternity is very long. This truth hit me as I hit my 40s. *What am I doing to make a difference? Why am I here? What is my desire?* I know this sounds like a midlife crisis, but it wasn't. I don't think so? But, I did buy a convertible three years ago! If it was a crisis, it was a healthy one. I questioned everything. I re-evaluated my life, and made a lot of changes to refocus.

As co-CEO of Shady Maple Companies, I help lead and cast vision for growth at all our entities including Shady Maple Smorgasbord, Farmers Market (supermarket), and others. We have the largest smorgasbord restaurant in the USA and the largest farmers market in Pennsylvania. We have an amazing, unique story that we desire to be a legacy.

Many people ask how our name came to be. Great question! My grandpa owned the land where the plaza is now located, and he was a farmer of local grown produce and tobacco. As an entrepreneur in his day, he decided to retail his produce under a very large maple tree in front of his house. As you can imagine, it was shady under the tree!

In 1970, my father took the entrepreneurial spirit to the next level by building the first Shady Maple Farmers Market. It was only 3,000 square feet with no air conditioning. Now, it is hard to imagine that was our beginning. In 2010, I spearheaded our 16th remodel and addition to this first store. That created our current 150,000 square foot store!

The history of Shady Maple is a fascinating story of desire, discipline, and determination. If you want the whole story, read the book *Under the Maple Tree* by my dad Marvin Weaver. We have so many stories of going through mountaintop experiences like growing sales almost every year of business to low valley experiences of needing to borrow money to make payroll and wondering if it was going to all work out.

Today, Shady Maple plaza is a very unique experience. Our average customer drives 30 miles one way to this destination. We make over 1000 different homemade recipes from scratch every week. This includes making by hand over three million donuts per year. Automated equipment is okay, but if you want the best, sometimes you need to do it the hard way. The plaza has an average of 50,000 diners and shoppers per week. The day before Mother's Day is always our busiest day. The restaurant serves up to 11,000 meals that day alone. This orchestrated production for all business entities takes over 800 hard-working employees.

I was born into an amazing Christian family. They always demonstrated agape love and taught us so much about life. I am now married with four wonderful children. From as early as I can remember, I always had the entrepreneurial spirit. I constantly was thinking about how I could create revenue, and I had multiple ventures from selling puppies when I was six years old to planting three acres of pumpkins and watermelons at age 21. I wish I had pictures of my wife and me planting that field by hand as newlyweds. By the way, the watermelons were an epic failure! The few watermelons I did harvest tasted awful from lack of due diligence before planting. The pumpkins on the other hand did great! I will never forget the feeling of finishing my P&L after the pumpkin season was over and clearing a $3000 net profit. I know that doesn't sound like much, but when you have an idea you see through, and you invest sweat and tears, you celebrate any victory you can! I grew up in the family business. Some of my earliest memories were tagging along with my mom as she merchandised produce for sale in the store. I started punching a clock at age 13 and worked in many areas throughout the businesses. I still work at Shady Maple full-time.

When I hit 40, I started wondering: *What are we doing now that will last longer than ourselves? What is fulfilling for each person's life?* If you find your purpose, then desire, discipline, and determination will follow. I think many people die and never find this for their life. So sad! I have found part of this for my life, but I am still learning and discovering all the reasons God put me on Earth.

Part of my DNA inherited from my grandpa is a generous spirit. My grandpa was so generous, he could not even pass a hitchhiker without picking him up and taking him the extra mile, literally. Like my grandpa, I too love to add value to others. My wife and I had the opportunity to volunteer at a safe home in Nepal for people rescued out of human sex trafficking. We also have countless stories of helping employees that have health crises or unexpected expenses through life's ups and downs. My wife Bernice will even take meals to people's houses and pray with them if they are open to that. I believe that whoever gives the most hope has the most influence in life!

What do we desire at Shady Maple? All people are born with a desire to belong, a desire to be part of something bigger than ourselves. Money is important, but money never brought anyone true joy and contentment. You run faster alone and farther with a team. Even the most successful person on Earth is empty inside without purpose. I think of the time Carol, who works in the produce department, went around asking coworkers to give money to help a coworker going through a financial hardship. Seeing people show kindness for each other even when it is not part of their job description is priceless to me.

What makes Shady Maple lasting? Successful people *implement* brilliant ideas, not just have brilliant ideas. I think the most lasting thing in the restaurant and grocery industry is creating smiles. If we can get guests to smile, it is a victory! The people that work at Shady Maple are truly the reason Shady Maple is successful.

Another reason for our success is the wow factor. We always say, "Stack it high, watch it fly." People shop with their eyes first. We make big, fancy displays, and always keep quality number one with reasonable prices. During the summer, we make two three-foot wide and 50 lb. mango habanero cheeseburgers over charcoal, cut them up, and give them away as samples just for anyhow! We have employees from competitors come shop at Shady Maple companies on a regular basis, and this is fun feedback that we must be doing something right.

Our biggest way to leave lasting value is to honor every employee and guest entering the plaza by creating experiences of joy and celebration. Trust me, this is not always easy. Some people are very challenging! From the customer I saw take a bite out of a daikon and put it back on the shelf to the customer yelling and screaming mad because we ran out of bacon at the buffet for 10 minutes (by the way we have over 10 other meats to pick from). People can be challenging. It is our job to meet them where they are. We don't know their story. They might have just lost a loved one or be coming through a crisis. I enjoy talking to customers with complaints. I know I am a little strange, but dissolving the situation and creating a win-win is so rewarding. But, the saying "The customer is always right," is not true! 1-2% of our customers we wish we could fire. I think some people have a goal in life to cause problems. The flip side is we do many things to have fun with employees and customers. This includes events like Midnight Gladness where we are open to midnight two days before Christmas with great sale prices and all kinds of sampling. We even bring in strobe lights and Christmas carolers. Last year, it was so busy we ran out of parking spaces at 10 p.m. Another unique thing we do is close the whole plaza every Sunday for workers and customers to have time for family and to worship if they desire. Yes, this is the biggest revenue day of the week, but we feel it is worth it.

I believe in doing whatever it takes to make a difference. In life, sometimes you need to sacrifice. Sometimes you need to do things that make your stomach hurt. Your comfort zone will be your coffin. I love learning. I even recently started attending some events put on by The Real Estate Guys to learn about investing. Leaders are learners. Casualness will lead to causality. Be willing to do whatever it takes to get through the day. We are so willing to not disappoint customers, we will go to great extremes. Last year before Christmas, two employees at Shady Maple, Bal and Connie, worked a 22-hour shift one day making donuts just so we wouldn't run out!

Let's talk about how taking offence affects our legacy. Are you willing to hold grudges? One thing I inherited from my dad was the ability to forgive and forget. I remember one time an employee said something very disparaging about him. A week later, Elwood, our store manager, said, "What are you going to do about this?" and my dad did not remember it had happened. When you feel hurt, it is okay. That is normal. But what is the next step? Choose to forgive and be concerned about the offender's best interests. If you go to them with that mentality, you are three quarters of the way to resolution and restoration. In life, I guarantee you there will be lots of conflict. The more you are in charge of, the more opportunity for misunderstandings.

Do you know the lasting impact of your words? Part of our Shady Maple values is to speak life. There is more power in your words than you realize. Imagine throwing a stone in a lake and watching the ripples go out. That is like every one of your words. Good or bad, they go out and create influence. Every day, I pray and speak the words for what I want to see manifest in our lives and business.

Is what's inside of you able to withstand time? If you want to know, think back to some of your most stressful times and what came out of you. For some of us it is lack of patience. I remember when I planted seeds in my pumpkin field. I waited and waited for the plants to grow, and I saw nothing. Fear set in, and I asked my wife, "What went wrong?" I dug up some plants to see, and they were within a centimeter of breaking through the ground!

Shady Maple is an example of success through discipline. Daily, many mundane tasks must be done with excellence. This takes a lot of healthy people working in unity. People without healthy habits become frustrated with life. Create time for what is important. We all have 86,400 seconds per day to plan our repetition which will by default become your reputation. For me, faith, family, friends, finance, fun, and fitness are my core values in that order. If they do not have space in each day, my personal equilibrium is off balance. Faith in God is more important than anything else. We are on Earth to worship Him and bring Heaven to Earth. That is another book.

There is more power in association than you realize. Social capital is the most important thing in the world. Like it or not, you will become like who you hang out with. Build relationships with people that are where you want to be in the future: people that inspire you. I think of Jerry Horst, a local real estate developer and builder who authored a chapter in *Purpose, Passion & Profit*. Every time I am with him, I leave a better person than before. He has a gift of believing in you and speaking encouraging words.

Lastly, make time for healthy fun and fitness. Laughing 100 times a day is like running 10 miles for your heart. One thing I do to stay in shape is play racquetball. It is time to get a healthy diet, a no drama diet. Don't let negative drama consume you! Turn off the news. Turn off the TV. Plug into things that speak life. In our pharmacy, we sell a lot of depression and anxiety medication. I understand some of this cannot be prevented because of chemical imbalances and other situations, but I believe a lot could be helped by healthy habits of speaking words of life out loud over our lives and opening our ear and eye gates only to things that are life-giving. If you complain, you remain.

What will be the Shady Maple legacy? Last year in one of my coaching sessions with our emerging leaders program, I said, "Take 15 minutes and write your obituary." It was eye-opening for many of them to think about what others will remember them for. It is important to realize none of us are getting out of here alive. We can decide now, daily, how that newspaper paragraph will be written. Think. How long is eternity? Does what we do have meaning beyond our lifetime? I hope Shady Maple will be a place of opportunity, a place that fought for kindness, a place that appreciates people's talents. We are all smart in the way we are created. Everyone is a very important person. You were created for a reason. I remember when my firstborn Lindsey was learning to walk. She was clumsy and awkward, but when she took that first step on her own, my heart was about to explode with joy. Every year I realize more this is how our Heavenly Father feels about you every day! His heart is exploding with love and pride for you. God is posting pics of you on heavenly Facebook right now saying "Did you see that? Ain't that the cutest thing you ever saw? Ain't that amazing?!"

The Shady Maple history was not a get rich quick scheme. Whenever I hear someone promote an easy way to make quick money, I'm disgusted. Wealth takes time, hard work, pain, and diligence. Life is often hard. We all have regrets. Running a business is not easy. Unexpected things like soaring healthcare costs can destroy budgets in one month completely out of the blue. Do things that last. Invest in people. Don't partner with people you don't trust just because the money looks good. Set your portfolio up with a 200 year mindset. In the early stage of Facebook, the founder was offered 100 million dollars. He turned it down. Sell out for your purpose.

The Shady Maple mission is "serving all with honor and integrity." We are all called to serve. What are you serving? Yourself? I found that is a recipe for very short-term happiness. Living to make a difference, now that's something to get excited about! Doing things that help others, those are the things I look back on and treasure the memories. A legacy worth living and dying for!

TWEETABLE
If you are not stretching, you are not growing.

Lin Weaver and his wife, Bernice, along with their four children live in East Earl, PA. His drive and success in business is fueled by his passion to serve people. He serves on local boards and partners with international nonprofits.

For more information about Shady Maple or to just to get to know each other, (Proverbs 27:17) please contact Lin at Lweaver@shady-maple.com or www.shady-maple.com

CHAPTER 12

Tell Richard Branson, Charles Schwab, Steve Jobs, Henry Ford, Ted Turner that a Learning Disability Will Hold Them Down

by Michael Buffington

Who fails kindergarten?

I failed kindergarten! Yes...that's right. This is a class where I was learning to write my name, have snacks, take naps, and color with crayons. How hard could it be?

I never really liked school and usually felt overwhelmed and frustrated. In grade school I never understood why it seemed so hard. When my parents held me back in kindergarten, they didn't have a grasp of what was going on either. I didn't hate school, I just always knew I found things harder than most of the other students.

It turns out, I have a learning disability, and my brain processes the way I hear and see words a little differently than most. I don't recall when I realized I had a learning disability or if I even really cared at the time. I certainly don't care anymore.

At some point, the school I was attending realized I needed a little extra help. In fifth grade, they assigned a special teacher to help me in some of my classes and provide one-on-one tutoring. I found this extremely embarrassing at the time and often put my head down in shame for needing the extra help. Today, I realize we all need coaching and some extra help at some point.

I remember when one teacher in high school told me I would never amount to anything. This is hard to hear from an educator. You start to wonder if they are right, and it can pull you down even further. Fortunately, I never let her seed of negativity grow in my head. I now know I was not making life easy for her in her class, and she was just trying to find a way to deal with me.

While I was struggling with my learning disability, the rest of my life wasn't always easy either. I don't say this looking for pity because I know there are others out there that have a much more difficult life than me, and I know if we learn from our struggles and difficulties in life, it makes us stronger. By the time I was 18, my parents had been divorced for years, my mother was admitted to the hospital several times to be treated for a mental illness, and my brother struggled with his own mental illness and substance abuse, which led to him taking his girlfriend's life and then his own.

I do need to mention, my parents were always loving, caring, and supportive of me even during our family turmoil. There are some things I wish we could roll back, but we all make mistakes, and it's learning from those mistakes that make us and those around us stronger. I am extremely grateful that my parents instilled in me a very strong work ethic and encouraged my entrepreneurial spirit in a loving and caring way. It is important we show our kids that we love, care, and support them, especially when things are difficult.

Fortunately, I didn't have problems with everything in school. Although I normally bombed any test that required writing out an answer, I actually enjoyed and did well (most of the time) in math, science, and any hands-on class.

Today, I often use work and projects as therapy when I need a mental break from something that is bothering me. There's nothing like some physical labor and getting your hands dirty to give yourself some time to reflect. After my parents separated, I spent countless hours taking care of the 10 plus acres that I lived on with my mother. We also had new neighbors, Jim and Nancy Ryan, who bought the farm across the street to start a nursery. Jim and Nancy didn't have any kids of their own then, but they had hearts of gold and treated me like their own child. I had so much fun helping Jim build his nursery on his property.

Jim would become my first business partner in fourth grade. He was a very talented florist and could make spectacular arrangements. On a handshake, we created a Christmas business where I sold Christmas trees and arrangements out of a shed on our property along with an order and delivery option for some surrounding businesses. Jim would buy all the material and inventory for our business and create arrangements. I would sell them with any free time I had during the week and on the weekends. After all expenses, we would split the profits; Jim would get 60%, and I took the remaining 40%. Our second (and final) year, I don't remember the exact amount we profited, but it was in the thousands of dollars. I felt like the richest kid around. I will always be grateful that Jim sparked my interest in business and partnerships so early in life.

After graduating high school (I was worried I wouldn't for a while), I decided not to go to college right away. My original plan was to take a year off from school and then try to determine what I wanted to do. Besides, I knew if I went to college at that time I would spend more time partying than studying. I went full-time with my high school job at a local building supply company, but only for a short time before meeting Bob Lepley, one of the people who changed the course of my life.

Bob was a neighbor of mine in high school and only lived a couple of doors away from me, but I didn't get to know him until he pulled me aside at work and offered me a position at his electrical supply and contracting business. Originally, he hired me to help organize and set-up a computer system for his inventory. I didn't work for him long before he took me under his wing and started teaching me I could do anything I applied myself to. Eventually, I was estimating and providing project management to all kinds of projects, including million dollar projects. He had me meeting with professionals (engineers, architects, attorneys, accountants, etc.) who were much more educated than I was. But Bob was the first person to tell me just because they had more education than I, didn't mean I could not be successful.

While working for him, I ended up buying my first rental property at the age of 18 just up the street from his office. Without his encouragement, I don't think I would have ever purchased this property. This would end up being the start of my real estate investing.

I ended up working for Bob for almost two years. I looked up to him as a father. He was smart, had a very successful business, and also invested in some real estate. I could never truly thank Bob for all the lessons I learned about business and real estate working under him. He pushed me into the path of being a real estate and business owner and investor.

When I left Bob's company in 1995, this would be the last real job I would ever have. Although, after much personal and professional development I realize I was young and dumb and wouldn't leave for the same reasons now, I do not regret it. Leaving ended up opening doors in my life I didn't even know existed. I do regret the loss of Bob's true friendship. Knowing what I know today, I would have handled the situation differently.

Shortly after leaving Bob's business, I worked some odd jobs and started my own business doing electrical work and business phone systems. I still did not have a clear direction in my life, but with the confidence Bob instilled in me, I was not afraid to tackle any project or business idea. My best friend's father introduced me to one of his high school friends in the wireless phone business. I could never have imagined where this door would lead. At that time most wireless phones were either installed in vehicles or in a big bag. It would be a few more years until handheld phones started to become the norm. But this opportunity would turn out to be the biggest business opportunity of my life to date.

This introduction eventually led me to form One-Stop Communications in 1996. We started with a retail store in Lewistown, Pennsylvania selling wireless phones, satellite systems, and other communications products. This business is still in operation today and thriving with several locations in central Pennsylvania. Over the last 22 years, this business has transformed several times as consumer demands have changed, technology has evolved, markets have changed, and new opportunities have been created. The success of this business would not be possible without all the great people who are involved and their willingness to change.

Just like people, every business must be willing to adapt as we grow and as our surroundings and circumstances change. Those not willing to change will be stuck, no longer growing, and just maybe, dying. Think about all those people and businesses you know of that were not willing to adapt and change. I bet most of those businesses eventually fail.

This business started because I quit my job and I was introduced to one person in the wireless phone industry. Once that door opened, we became a multimillion-dollar business. We have worked with several Fortune 500 companies and have been recognized by them as an award-winning organization for sales and customer service. This did not happen overnight, and we have had our ups and downs, but desire, discipline, and determination from everyone at One-Stop Communications has made us a great organization.

During this journey of building and creating a great business, I discovered the power of personal and professional development. It was almost a necessity for me to figure out how to build and grow this business. I starting reading and listening to books about personal and professional development, and over time, more doors continued to open. To this day, reading is still a struggle. When you become successful your disabilities don't go away. I did learn to enjoy reading, but that doesn't mean I need to be able to pronounce every word in the English language (something I struggle with). As long as I understand the meaning, I get the benefit.

As I read more books, I learned more and more about business, investing, and personal improvement. I acquired a few properties through my twenties, but I never truly understood how to invest and manage real estate until I started reading about real estate investing and management. I even sold my first rental property after some experiences that made me wonder why anyone would want to own rental properties and swore I would never be a landlord again. Now I own residential, commercial, and mixed-use properties that cash flow enough for me to live comfortably. I continue to reinvest most of what I make in real estate to build real wealth for my family.

Rich Dad Poor Dad by Robert Kiyosaki was one of the first books I ever read that changed the way I think. Robert's book is easy to read and understand. Plus, his message that A and B students work for C students ignited a fire in me. Guess what, I was a C student. Be sure to study and understand Kiyosaki's cashflow quadrants.

I have not stopped reading and learning. I still make mistakes on a regular basis. The key is to identify your mistakes, learn from them, and take action to avoid the same mistakes in the future. I always remind myself and those working with me "*inaction = failure.*" Be sure to take action or you will fail. Go ahead: don't call your customers back, don't work on your business, don't work on your marriage, ignore those tax bills, don't review financial reports, don't go to the doctor. I hope you get the point here. If you fail to take action, you will never get started, and you are guaranteed to fail.

If you want to be truly successful in life, learn to solve problems. The more and the larger the problems you learn to solve for others, the more successful you will be. These problems can be real or perceived. There are millionaires out there that have solved the perceived problem of cleaning toilets. Most of us can and know how to clean a toilet, but we don't want to (perceived problem, not real). So we hire cleaners to take care of cleaning them for us. Every business and life is filled with problems, and it is up to us to always be solving problems for ourselves, our loved ones, our employees, our peers, and our customers.

In my own life, I had to learn how to overcome my learning disability. It still exists to this day and is very real—something I cannot ignore. I use others to help me solve this problem when needed. My wonderful wife will get emails from me on a regular basis asking her to proofread something I have written. She is always extremely busy, so when I have a larger project I will hire a proofreader. I also use technology to overcome minor proofreading. Problem solved.

I am so fortunate to have so many wonderful people in my life from my family, friends, employees, partners, and those I work with on a regular basis. It is important to keep yourself surrounded by good, honest people. With the right people and the right attitude, you can achieve just about anything. I have made deliberate effort to remove or distance myself from those with a negative attitude.

None of this matters if you don't have the right attitude. Attitude is the one thing we have total control over in our lives. No one else controls our attitude. You have a choice of how you are going to react to anything thrown at you in life. The wrong attitude will quickly break any family, business, or organization. We truly are a product of our attitude. I believe life is 10% of what happens to us and 90% how we react to it. You are in charge of your attitude!

Gratitude is attitude. Once you find those people and opportunities in life, be thankful for them and all they do. It is easy to get caught up in our days and forget what we should be thankful about. Take some time to reflect on those problems that have created opportunities. Take some time to thank those in your life. Sometimes a smile and a few kind words are all it takes. Remember you are in charge of your attitude and gratitude is attitude.

Those with learning disabilities see the world a little differently and often find a better way to solve problems. Go ahead tell Richard Branson, Charles Schwab, Steve Jobs, Henry Ford, Ted Turner or the thousands of other successful people out there that their learning disability will hold them down. You are in charge of your life and it is up to you to overcome and solve any of life's challenges.

TWEETABLE

If you want to be truly successful in life, learn to solve problems. The more and the larger the problems you learn to solve, the more successful you will be and sometimes those problems are our own struggles and disabilities.

As a business and real estate investment specialist, Michael Buffington purchased his first property just out of high school and before age 23 founded a successful retail company that now operates multiple locations throughout Pennsylvania. He oversees several companies that manage commercial and residential investment properties. He continues to build his portfolio of businesses and real estate investments through partnerships while exploring ways to help others overcome their struggles and learning disabilities. To connect with Mike for investment, partnerships or consulting opportunities email: mike@michaelbuffington.com

Visit www.michaelbuffington.com for additional bonus material and to stay connected with Mike.

CHAPTER 13

Tap Those ASSets

Emerging from 'Prison' to Becoming an Entrepreneur, Investor, and Savings Passionista

by L. Tia Blount

"When I grow up, I want to be *visible*," I would mumble inaudibly. Strange coming from a five-year-old girl. Typically, at that age, thoughts turn to becoming a doctor, lawyer, or even a princess. I was born in the late 70s and raised by a single parent in a low-income household in southeast Washington, DC. During those days—many fell victim to the crack cocaine epidemic in the District—either becoming users or dealers, an inevitable fate that didn't appear to be open to revision, and where both sides met disastrous ends.

My mother worked tirelessly to move us out of "the projects." Those long work hours often translated into nights, or even weeks, at my grandmother's house. My beloved grandmother was a mother of 14 children, a devoted missionary, and a pillar in the community. Under her roof, there were always people coming and going. They'd come to experience powerful, soul-stirring sermons from the small, makeshift church in her basement, and often leave with bags filled with clothing, toys, and other supplies received as donations for her nonprofit.

With so much movement in and out of my grandmother's home, I often went *unnoticed*, and so did my sexual abuse.

My environment reflected my mental and emotional outlook—underdeveloped and poverty-stricken. Inside my grandmother's home, family often slept three or four to a bed, roach infestations were commonplace, and food was boxed, canned, and scarce. Outside, the spattering of gunshots, the raucous shouts of drunkards staggering home, and the ballet of police sirens created an obnoxious urban symphony that made it impossible to sleep. Those long nights and silent cries were met with a burning desire for freedom from my environment and from undetected molestation at the hands of an older male relative.

With what little resources I had at my disposal, I eventually learned to tap into two of my earliest known ASSets: imagination and writing. Armed with a pen, paper, a vivid imagination and visualization—I would sit up for hours writing and constructing my future. I literally wrote my way out of this mental prison, out of my environment, into college, and into a career in global health communications. I'd go on to visit nearly 30 countries to experience the very images I had imagined during my childhood "time travels," a coping mechanism I unwittingly adopted to disassociate or minimize the emotional pain.

Early in my career I spent time building clinical trial networks and extending communications capacity across some of the most remote villages in Africa. I worked for two large NGOs whose missions were to accelerate the development of prevention technologies for HIV/AIDS and malaria respectively. My time outside of work was devoted to learning about personal finance, real estate, and investing. Having no formal education except for the in-home stock market courses taught by my dogged Vietnamese investment coach Hai Nguyen, I was determined to save (and eventually invest) every dollar I could. Tapping the ASSets of discipline and determination, I studied and crunched numbers, assembled and disassembled budgets, studied spending patterns, and learned to control unhealthy emotions around spending. Through monthly budget development and weekly tracking, I created a budgeting system that took me from $1 in savings to over $1500 a month. With the savings created, I began dabbling in the stock market, mostly through trial and error, and investing in several other ASSets including mutual funds and real estate.

Taking a slow, steady, and systematic approach, I grew $1 in savings to over a quarter of a million in ASSets in less than 10 years. I knew this was the kind of money and system that could change lives, particularly those who grew up in similar neighborhoods. I shared my system and created hundreds in monthly savings for individuals, couples, families, women's groups, and churches. I became a savings passionista (one with a passion and skill for savings), an avid investor, and a budget coach. I found an uncanny parallel in my ability to help organizations save time and money extending into the millions, on marketing and business solutions. I believe it was partly my ability to develop strategies, map critical paths, dissect budgets, and evaluate what was critical and what was fluff.

After a prosperous nine-year climb up the corporate ladder and establishing a home-based business devoted to budget coaching and debt elimination,

2008 hit like a tsunami, destroying everything in its path. For the next four years, my life was reminiscent of a town devastated by storm. I was left to rummage through the rubble to find what was left of any semblance of normalcy. My business suffered during the recession, my five years of marriage ended in divorce, and I was left to pay several mortgages that resulted in foreclosure proceedings on my primary residence. I lost my job in early 2012 due to funding shortages. To add insult to injury, my health was being challenged by a spinal disorder that limited my range of motion. I felt emotionally, physically, and mentally broken. The mental prison I thought I had escaped as a child was once again threatening me with steel bars and a powerful grip. I battled with depression and turned to alcohol and overeating as coping mechanisms. I settled into this pattern until a close colleague saw a familiar pain in my eyes and suggested I see a counselor. I reluctantly agreed although I wasn't convinced I had a problem.

My counselor diagnosed me with post-traumatic stress disorder and suggested a treatment plan. Sessions were grueling. We were able to unearth memories I thought I had laid to rest. I discovered that I had merely swept my traumas under the proverbial rug and pretended to function as normal. I often overcompensated in areas of my life (i.e., my career) to avoid the sense of powerlessness and fear I felt as a child. When faced with setbacks or "triggers," feelings that lay dormant and unresolved rose to the surface.

Session after session, I separated what "happened" in my past from "the stories" I told myself. This myopic cognitive dissonance framed my beliefs about self, men in general, and my inability to trust. Once I channeled these negative emotions, I learned to release them and tap into the ASSet of positive thought. I applied the same desire, discipline, and determination to my mental, physical, and spiritual health as I had to my career and my finances. I incorporated rituals of prayer, meditation, scripture reading, journaling, exercise, and positive affirmations. I learned about my triggers and practiced healthy dialogue rather than becoming frustrated and reverting to unhealthy coping mechanisms. My process led to an increase in compassion, forgiveness, and a commitment to advocate for others who suffer in silence.

Ironically, this breakthrough in mind-body-spirit alignment resulted in a breakthrough in my career. In late 2012, I landed a gig as director of marketing for a Maryland-based real estate developer that preserves affordable housing and provides life-changing programs and services for low-to-moderate-income families. While going through my internal transformation, I managed to transform the culture of the organization in the process. During my six-year tenure, I created a new organizational culture, raised our visibility and profile, helped expand our real estate portfolio and geographic footprint, assisted in securing additional resources, and was promoted to vice president of external relations.

Day by day, one calculated step at a time, I rebuilt other areas of my life, including my credit and the remnants of dwindling ASSets that I had worked so hard to accumulate. With my mind, body, and spirit aligned through counseling, daily rituals, and with the help of chiropractic, acupuncture, and reiki (energy work) for my spine, I discovered the ASSets of wellness, balance, and confidence—ASSets that had only existed in principle up to this point.

By early 2017, the developer I worked for became such an attractive company that the CEO decided to merge with a national intermediary. He approached me to lead the due diligence and transition planning phases of the corporate merger, a process that would ultimately result in me firing myself and other support functions that were duplicated in the larger organization. After getting over the initial shock and disappointment, I tapped the ASSet of positive thought and decided to view this as an opportunity. I also tapped the ASSet of confidence to negotiate an aggressive retention package and took on a new role as chief of strategy charged with leading the transition.

Upon signing my walking papers at the end of 2017, I took a much-needed sabbatical to clear my head, ideate on next steps, and travel to eight countries. During this period of reflection and realignment, I tapped into my mentors as ASSets and sought guidance, encouragement, and wisdom. I had several conversations with my business mentor and good friend Ype Von Hengst, cofounder, COO, and vice president of culinary operations of Silver Diner, a successful restaurant chain across Maryland and Virginia. I reconnected with one of my real estate coaches Ronnie Lucas, an avid investor who introduced me to my first international real estate deal in Salvador Bahia, Brazil. I also met my newest mentor, Kyle Wilson, the mastermind behind Jim Rohn International and coauthor of *Chicken Soup for the Entrepreneur's Soul*. Kyle encouraged me and gave me a platform to share my story.

While abroad, I applied for several jobs, one of which resulted in an offer for a C-suite (chief marketing officer) position working in community development. While this opportunity would have been the normal career progression, my spirit spoke from a different place. I was tired of not standing in my full potential and allowing fear of uncertainty, criticism, and failure to have a grip on my life. Deep within my soul I could hear that five-year-old girl crying, this time loudly and audibly, "I want to be *VISIBLE*." This yearning is now translated as my desire to have an impact on those who feel helpless with respect to personal finance and those who want to increase their visibility and profitability in business.

In 2018, I tapped the ASSet of faith and transformed my fledgling consultancy initially established in 2012—one that took on clients on an ad-hoc basis—into a fully operational firm that blends my passion and purpose. I am now the founder of Saving Solutions, a boutique firm that specializes in saving individuals and businesses time and money on three powerful *solutions*: buzz marketing, business development, and budgeting. I continue to coach individuals, couples, and families on using my R.E.A.L.I.S.T.I.C. budget method, one that can create hundreds in monthly savings. I am also a real estate and novice stock market investor that started with nothing but the desire, determination, and discipline to break the poverty cycle, move beyond living paycheck-to-paycheck, and escape what Robert Kiyosaki refers to as the "rat race."

If you're wondering what this whole **ASSet** business is all about, now is where I give you the punch line. Over the years, I've discovered that ASSets are far greater than tangible possessions measurable in terms of money (i.e., stocks, bonds, mutual funds, real estate, gold, etc.). An ASSet can also be intangible (i.e., valuable qualities, characteristics, people, or resources). The capitalization of **"ASS" in ASSet**, as referenced throughout this chapter, is designed to be a subconscious signal that nothing happens in life without your ability to:

1) Discover valuable tangible and intangible ASSets that can be tapped,

2) Create a plan of action designed to put those ASSets to work for you, and

3) **Get your ASS-set in gear and do the work.**

While mine isn't the story of a multi-millionaire sharing the secrets to getting rich quick, I hope to inspire you to take action to improve your finances, starting first with a R.E.A.L.I.S.T.I.C. budget. I encourage you to plan for emergencies as we continue to experience shifts in the economy. I empower you to tap into intangible ASSets that help you break free of mental, emotional, and/or physical barriers that have (or may) come your way. Desire, discipline, and determination are among the main ASSets I tapped to emerge from my mental prison to become an entrepreneur, investor, and savings passionista.

What ASSets will you tap?

TWEETABLE

Nothing happens in life without your ability to 1) discover valuable tangible and intangible ASSets that can be tapped, 2) create a plan of action designed to put those ASSets to work for you, and 3) get your ASS-set in gear and do the work.

L. Tia Blount is founder of Saving Solutions, a firm specializing in saving you time and money on three powerful, high-impact solutions: buzz marketing, business development, and budgeting. L. Tia is a former corporate leader for a MD-based real estate development firm and spent nearly 10 years leading local and international communications efforts in HIV/AIDS and malaria. She is a passionate budget coach and spends time volunteering and coaching on her R.E.A.L.I.S.T.I.C. budget method—one that can create hundreds in monthly savings to support short-, medium- and long-term goals and can change your life.

Contact: To connect with L. Tia Blount for speaking engagements, for marketing and/or business development support, or to learn more about the R.E.A.L.I.S.T.I.C. budget method, visit www.savingsolutions.biz or send an email to savingsolutions1@gmail.com.

CHAPTER 14

The Legacy of the Comeback Kid

by Ed Myrick

He survived 12 heart attacks and strokes over the past 15 years. He even survived polio as a kid. Not once, but twice. He was made fun of and called "the cripple kid" in school, and he became the vice president of a Fortune 200 company by the time he was 30. He was a fighter and the comeback kid! However, I knew this time he would not make a big comeback. His heart was too weak to keep pumping for much longer.

At this point, the doctors had not told us that my father would not survive, but somehow I knew. I was working at the corporate office of a major financial institution. While at work pacing back and forth on the phone with my brother, it all became real. It also became obvious to me that I was going to have to quit my well-paying job with great benefits to care for my father and mother during his final months and beyond. This meant no more medical coverage or paychecks. It also meant depleting my savings to do the right thing.

The decision to leave work and oversee my father's healthcare was an easy one. I learned with his first heart attack, where he went into full cardiac arrest and had to be resuscitated, that family came first. I could always get another job, but not another father. I didn't tell him that I quit my job, but he knew because I was always with him and never at work.

At this point, he still did not realize he was not going to make it. The doctors told him, and so did we. But it was easier to live in denial than face the inevitable. I couldn't work and take care of my father and mother. They lived 45 minutes away on a good traffic day. Now that my father was sick, I had to start running his rental properties including the day to day operations. He was also an accountant and still had customers that depended on him. Luckily, I had been paying many of my parents' bills and property taxes and had been managing many of their affairs for the past 10 years.

His health continued to decline. On bad days when he breathed it sounded like he was gargling water. His heart was not strong enough for him to clear his airways of fluid. He was constantly panicking because he couldn't fill his lungs with air and feared he would suffocate. The doctors would give him medicine to help. But each time it was a temporary fix. All the while, he was looking at me or my mother to help, and we couldn't do anything. Looking back, we realized how much we did not understand how to help him physically. Even worse, we were terrible at offering emotional support. We simply did not understand what he was going through or how to help.

He did have a number of good days between the bad. God has a sense of humor. On his good days he would create unique challenges for me and fires I had to put out. My father was a CPA, and he was sick during the first quarter of 2013. On his good days, he would be on his cell phone calling his clients and talking about their taxes. He would also tell them that he was fine, and that he hadn't received their tax information yet. They had no idea how sick he was. I would hear these conversations and think to myself, *Crap! These people need to get their taxes done, and I am going to have to tell them the truth and to go elsewhere.* I later learned his plan was for me to do their taxes with him instructing me. I am still not sure what adjectives are appropriate to use here to explain how I felt about his plan.

Weeks of suffering turned into months, and he needed 24-hour care. We decided to keep him at home, so I hired caretakers to help. At this point, he had to be physically lifted off of the bed to move or change him. Moving him was always scary. He was becoming so frail, there was no way to move him without injuring him a little. His pain tolerance was depleted, and when you applied minimal pressure to his body, he felt like someone was hitting him. He was in pain, struggling to breathe, and we didn't know how to help. Imagine your child pleading for help and all you can do is look at their desperate eyes and say it's going to be alright, knowing that you both know you are lying to them.

The time finally came when we were out of options. We could not take care of him at home and had to place him in a rehab center. While there, he actually got better. They set milestones, and he met them. He thought he was going to beat this and be the comeback kid once again. He also thought if he met their milestones he would go home. When he found out that was not the case, he gave up and gave in to his fate. He had to be sedated a lot due to his struggles to breathe. It was more humane to let him sleep through the pain rather than panic and stress. Still, he was scared, and no one could help. His days and nights got turned around, and hallucinations would follow. Many nights he would call me at 3 or 4 in the morning saying he had been kidnapped or people were running through the hospital with guns trying to kill people. To him this was real.

One evening, he called saying his best friend was holding him hostage in his garage. I asked my dad to look around and tell me what he saw. He described his room perfectly. I said "Dad, you have not been kidnapped, you are in your room." He replied that his friend "built a replica in his garage and did a damn good job of it." He was not kidding, and this was not the end of me attempting to convince him he was safe in his room. I learned you can't talk sense into people going through what he was going through or help them understand it is a hallucination. The best thing you can do is assure them they are safe and loved.

Eventually, the day came when the rehab center said there was nothing else they could do, and it was time to take him home and place him in hospice. I called a family meeting, and once again, it was my responsibility to tell the family what was going to happen. Then it was my job to tell him. He took it well and gave me a thumbs up. He understood that I needed his support and blessing. He was the one dying and needing support. Instead, he was supporting me emotionally. He had some good days after coming home. But he only came to the family room one time to watch TV before he died. Even after I told him he was going on hospice care, he never wanted to talk about it and would actually say "Let's not talk about that." So we didn't. Even though there were so many loose ends we needed to discuss, we chose to respect his wishes.

In his last 24 hours of life, it was apparent to everyone that this was it. We called his brothers and sister along with extended family to come visit him. After they all left, my mother and I gave him permission to die. He struggled to apologize for mistakes he made, and nature started taking its course.

He must have returned for a moment after he passed to check on my mother and I. I was laying on their couch, and I had severe chest pains. I grabbed my chest panicking and got up. At the same time, I could hear my mother in her bedroom getting out of bed and grabbing her walker. She said for some reason she had to get up, and get up now. We walked into my father's room to a sleeping hospice nurse. My father was laying on his back, eyes closed, and finally out of pain. He was wearing an old, tattered, white t-shirt. I remember hearing my mother saying his name, "Oh, Ronnie," one time in a disappointed voice. She was disappointed that he was gone.

It may seem odd to people who have never experienced death how comforting it is to be with your loved one after they have passed. I experienced this same comforting feeling a year and a half later when my mother passed away. I stayed with my father for a few hours until the funeral home arrived. You have the chance to talk, cry, and share with them before they are taken away.

When you are in charge of someone's health as their life comes to an end, it is a thankless job. My siblings were supportive of me while my father was going through the process. However, I don't think they ever understood the sacrifices, emotional toll, and guilt that comes with making decisions that affect so many. When you are the caretaker of a terminally ill parent, you will make mistakes, but you are doing **the best you know how.**

While caring for my parents, I learned who I am and what is important, and today I am able to sleep at night. I know I was there to see them through the end which gives me peace because they know I cared! I only wish they would have lived to meet my son Rhett who was born May 1, 2018. They would have loved him so much.

When you are the steward of other people's money, it is a a big responsibility that cannot be taken lightly. My parents instilled in me a spirit of entrepreneurship, accountability, and ethics that still hold true today. I have tried to make my parents proud my entire life. In their afterlife, I hope I continue to make them proud.

My parents understood the value of hard work, integrity, and the value of a dollar. Growing up poor, they wanted to give us more than they had. They also wanted us to work for our money and learn how to make it grow with savings and investments. That's why they owned about 50 units at one time in Irving, Texas. I have taken all they taught me and have ramped it up a few levels with apartment investing and syndicating. They may be gone, but their lessons will always drive me to be a better person and do the right thing. Losing them forced me to move out of my comfort zone and take calculated risks. In nine short months I was able to become a general partner on a 140-unit apartment complex in Memphis, Tennessee. I also invested in a lifestyle community in Wylie, Texas where people work, live, and play. This is completely out of my comfort zone because right now it is dirt, pipes, and concrete slabs. Soon you will see first-class apartments, retail stores, and restaurants. My mid-life crisis has nothing to do with slowing down. I am just getting started! Come join me—it is going to be a great journey!

TWEETABLE

They knew how much I cared. I held their hands and their hearts until they quit beating. This gives me peace. When you are the caretaker of a terminally ill parent, you will make mistakes, but you are doing the best you know how.

Ed Myrick owns Multifamily Capital and is an apartment syndicator and investor who is helping create financial freedom for himself and his real estate investors. Ed spent more than ten years in TV news doing every job in the newsroom from reporting the news and anchoring newscasts to managing news teams. He also spent close to ten years jet-setting across the country three weeks out of each month in the financial sector as a consultant and motivational speaker. Ed bought his first rental property with his father in 1988 and helped run the properties until 2018 when he started Multifamily Capital.

To hear how Ed can help secure your financial future or speak at one of your events, drop him an email at ed@multifamilycapital.com

Or visit his website at www.multifamilycapital.com

To laugh at him looking silly with his pride and joy visit https://www.facebook.com/ed.myrick

Find him on Linkedin at https://www.linkedin.com/in/ed-myrick-8ab73129/

CHAPTER 15

The One Thing That May Save Your Business

by Rachid Zahidi

There I was, in a remote area of Morocco, an area where good phone reception and internet were still scarce. There was only enough reception for me to receive a call that left me stressed out and unable to be present and enjoy where I was visiting.

I was in transit over the Atlas Mountains on my way to see my mom for my once a year visit. We both look forward to it, but she especially does as a mom who saw her son leave for another country over 25 years ago. You know how moms always worry, regardless of their children's age.

On this call, I found out payroll didn't go through, and a couple of big clients were late on payments. On top of that, a couple of key vendors stopped working, which created a backlog in work and services. The chain of challenging events ultimately drove one of my key managers to resign. Each development compounded my worry, anguish, and anxiety, especially because I was so far away. This was one of the worst periods in my entrepreneurial journey, even considering I had started the business from home a few years before with very limited resources and no employees. I had bootstrapped the business in the beginning, maxing out my credit cards and cashing out my 401k. I did the whole ramen noodle thing you hear about, all with a family to support.

When I got the phone call, it seemed like the sky was falling and I could lose everything I had worked for up to this point. The stress manifested in many ways in my body and my mind. This needed more than a quick call to fix.

How could this happen to our company? This was a company that had been named in many fast growth lists and that had been recognized as one of the fastest-growing companies, managing multiple employees and hundreds of independent contractors and researchers across the United States. It was a company which had and continues to screen millions and millions of employees and whose CEO has been featured on TV and radio shows,

Inc.com, and other industry publications. The truth was, as every entrepreneur knows, crises like this happen to many businesses, and the difference between who sticks with it and who is prepared for the roller coaster is desire, discipline, and determination.

As the adage goes, success is a poor teacher. Even though my team and I worked hard to achieve our initial success and the accolades that came with it, the fact is, the percentage of businesses, even with teams that work very hard, which make it past two years is very small. The percentage of businesses which make it past a million dollars in revenue is also small. We crossed that threshold back in 2011 and never looked back except to learn and gain perspective. We were honored to be featured in the local business journal as one of the fastest-growing companies, coming in at number seven only a few years after starting, and we were honored to be named a finalist in *Grow Florida's* "Companies to Watch" a couple of years later.

I must admit, it felt good to receive all the recognition and attention, but I also learned not to let success get to our heads as an organization or to my own head as an individual. As a matter of fact, when I am asked to speak to other entrepreneurs or contribute to publications, most often I will mention discipline and humility among other important qualities and core values.

To keep perspective, we have instilled the discipline to check our decision-making against certain criteria. The point is to avoid vanity-type decisions. When you find success, there are people great at stroking your ego to sell you stuff you don't need and many other temptations on which to blow your budgets. I have learned that if you don't have the determination to go uncover bad news or trouble areas early and at the source in your business, they will keep getting louder and will be loudest by the time they reach you as the owner or CEO.

When things are going great, there is a risk of expense creep. There is risk of inflated salaries or random hiring with no clear logic, goals, expectations, or accountability. It is the business equivalent of keeping up with the Joneses. I have since disciplined myself to stick to lessons previously learned and avoid big budget and ego tickling advertisements without specific measurable returns. I learned to verify and inspect what I expect when it comes to employees and vendors. It is also key to remember, as the adage goes, revenue is vanity, profit is sanity, and cash flow is reality.

With a couple of clients going bankrupt and a big account not collectable, we had reached the point where most declare bankruptcy. Our saving grace was all the goodwill we had built over the years with vendors and clients and the strength of those relationships. The character built from all my prior experiences, my upbringing, struggles, and challenges, allowed us to reach out to clients and vendors. We asked for and received their help and cooperation. Some clients paid us sooner than the agreed to terms, and some vendors extended longer terms than originally agreed upon. This provided enough cash flow to weather the storm and allow me to complete my trip.

When I got back to the US, we embarked on drastic cost-cutting measures including reducing unnecessary office space, re-negotiating pricing with vendors, and even re-negotiating some debts. We also asked for and received temporary extensions and lower payment requirements from the banks. Overall, we rolled up our sleeves and worked harder than we had in years. Determined, I dove back in personally and temporarily did the type of front-line work that I normally delegated, which allowed me to make things even more efficient. Also key was having a management trainee who was already being groomed for succession and able to help fill the void.

We did what most others who impacted us negatively didn't do. We didn't dodge the responsibility. I also sought advice from someone who had more gray hairs than I did. I leaned on my peer groups such us my EO Forum for advice, counsel, and sanity checks.

Most people responded, worked with us, and understood. As a reward, they kept our business relationship to this day. Things did get better eventually, and we learned a lot of lessons. Jumping back into the front lines allowed me to uncover inefficiencies and departures from our core values. As I was triaging and fixing these issues, I was reminded of my early days when I was fired up by being fed up with the corporate world, it's politics, and the bureaucracy. I had a deep desire to take control of my destiny. One of my main motivations for founding my company was to be able to spend time with my kids and go visit my parents and family overseas. While being an entrepreneur comes with a lot of responsibilities, it allowed me to decide when to do what and where. I have been able to visit family overseas once a year and at times more often than that.

I remember one occasion when this mattered most. I had just come back from overseas. Upon hearing that my dad was not doing well, I turned right back to be beside him. I would not have been able to pull off that trip if I were still working in the corporate world, especially back in those days. I was able to go back and spend time next to him and say a proper farewell before he passed a few years ago.

Now, don't get me wrong. When I am abroad I am still checking in and monitoring the company. I answer questions from my team at different times of the day, but I decide when and from where. As I look back and reflect on one of these most difficult periods in my entrepreneurial journey, I am grateful for the lessons, wisdom, and insights acquired.

The key to keeping it together is sticking with it and not throwing in the towel. Don't let what you can't do distract you from what you can do, and focus on what you can control. That is, rely on good processes and procedures and best practices rather than pinning your hopes on one star employee or any other single point of failure.

Keep moving forward. Learn from the mistakes, but don't dwell on them or let them define you. If you learn from them and they make you better and hardier, then it's not a total loss. Take the benefit of hindsight and turn it into foresight by facing challenges with the question: What is this here to teach me?

Remember for whom, for what, and why you are doing what you are doing. Be crystal clear about it. It will get you through the tough times.

Review your activities and tie them to their related results, then take out any that are getting you in trouble. My favorite business philosopher Jim Rohn said, "Success is nothing more than a few simple disciplines practiced every day." So, inspired by this quote, ask yourself as I do: If I keep repeating today, what will my week be like? What will my month look like? What will my year look like? And eventually, what will my legacy look like?

TWEETABLE
Years of building relationships with vendors and clients allowed my company to avoid bankruptcy. Relationships matter! Take care of yours.

Rachid Zahidi is an entrepreneur, author, speaker, and podcaster. He is CEO of Sentinel Background Checks and a University of Tampa graduate. His work experience spans multiple industries including risk management, background checks, international business, and anti-money laundering investigations. He is also the bestselling author of The Business Immunity System – The Pitfalls & Side Effects of Data Handling, Privacy Issues & Background Checks. Mr. Zahidi also served as finance chair then forum chair of the Central Florida chapter of Entrepreneur Organization. He has been featured on CLTV Chicago, Fox Baltimore, Inc.com, Florida Trend, The Background Buzz, Octane Magazine, ESPN Radio, and numerous other programs and publications discussing due diligence and information security related topics. Follow his blog https://rzspot.wordpress.com/ or Instagram @rachidpodcaster

Call at 813-381-5145 or email at rachid@sbchecks.com

CHAPTER 16

Fear Not

by Christine Brown-Kindred

Have you ever experienced **fear**? Not the fear from a horror movie or a thrill ride. I'm talking about the fear that stops you dead in your tracks. The fear of not being able to ask for what you really want. The fear of not taking a step to change your life. The fear of rejection that holds you back. The self doubt that might hold you back from opportunities that come your way. How about the fear of failure or fear of **success**?

The fear of both failure and success had me frozen in time.

I was living a life of fear. Always wanting to be accepted. Worried about what people thought of me. Saying yes to things, when I really didn't want to, to please others. Never wanting to be left behind. What was I going to miss?

I started a career as a hairstylist. It seemed to be the perfect fit, making clients feel good about themselves. It was a career designed to help others. I thought I had found my true passion. I did, but it wasn't the art of hairstyling. It was people. I loved my interaction and the relationships I had with my clients. As time passed, I found myself on a hamster wheel going nowhere fast. My career had taken a toll on me physically, and I needed to make a change.

I was desperate to find another career path and started using the resources I had at my fingertips, my clients—one client in particular, Todd Stottlemyre. Todd was a former Major League pitcher. I actually didn't know Todd as a baseball player. I had come to know Todd as a successful businessman and entrepreneur. I had such a respect for his accomplishments and his constant thirst for knowledge. I relied on him to teach me everything he knew.

He called one evening to have me come take a look at a business he was getting involved with. I couldn't drive to his home fast enough. He introduced me to network marketing. It truly was the last business I expected to see. I thought to myself that "those companies" never work! The business model made sense, and I had enough trust in Todd and his due diligence that I agreed to partner with him. To be quite honest, I had such fear of loss, that I was afraid not to do this.

By the next morning, that fear of loss had changed dramatically to: what are people going to think about me doing network marketing? How would I make this work? Would anyone find this to be a tangible business? I had convinced myself that I could start this business without having to tell any of my friends what I was doing. I had bought others' opinions that network marketing doesn't work before ever really taking the time to understand that network marketing companies offer products and services that allow you to build your own business. It is up to each individual to create their success.

I started working with Todd and was starting to see some success. I say some, because I was not fully committed to the process. I was very selective of the people I shared my opportunity with. I spent months without some of my closest friends knowing what I was doing. That fear of rejection sat in the back of my mind, and I allowed it to control my effort.

Six months into my new journey, I had the opportunity to spend the weekend with the founders of our company. That weekend, I was able to capture the vision of what I could really create if I worked hard. My clock was ticking at the salon, and I was determined to make this work! I spent that weekend learning everything I would need to return home and build a business.

I scheduled an evening, in my home, to share my opportunity. I was on a mission and started calling everyone I knew. I invited successful professionals, business owners, and those friends I was hiding from.

I included my good friend, John. John and I had known each other since early childhood and had an incredible friendship. About a year prior to this evening, John had suffered from a heart attack that led to a triple bypass. Besides his immediate family, I was his first call, and I was by his side at the hospital and throughout his recovery. I tell you this because, of all the people that were coming, I knew I would be able to count on John for support. I knew, no matter what, he would be so pleased that I had found a way out of the salon.

The big night was here. My newfound confidence had turned into knots in my stomach. I felt that I was about to face judgement from my peers. My thoughts were allowing my fear to take control, even though I believed that I had my hands on the most compelling business. My guests arrived, and my opportunity was presented. My nerves were unraveling. I looked to John for the support I thought he would offer. To my dismay, I looked to find him with his arms crossed, staring at the ceiling. I couldn't get past the boredom he clearly expressed.

I had some great responses that evening, and several people did see value in our company and wanted to immediately start working with our team. Even with the success, I couldn't embrace the positive because I was so focused on John's actions. I was devastated and relieved the night was over.

That night changed my life forever. I woke the next morning to find myself angry. I thought I was angry with my friend and his behavior. I wasn't. I was angry with myself because I had been allowing fear to control my life. Why was I expecting validation from others? My life was mine to design and people were always going to have their opinions. Worrying about opinions and judgement kept me a hostage. What about what I really wanted? What about my future? What about my dreams? The reality was, I hadn't been dreaming at all. Somehow my dreams got lost while riding the hamster wheel.

I turned my emotion into a burning desire that kept me moving forward and never looking back. I turned to my coach, Todd, for advice to keep my internal flame alive. He encouraged me to read. Books about others that have had to overcome incredible obstacles to win. I found within these books wisdom that I could apply daily. These words I was consuming provided me with the personal armor to take on any obstacle I might face. Those authors became my coaches that pushed me through adversity.

Seven months after that evening, I was finally presented with an opportunity to retire from the salon. With hard work, consistency, and a "No Quit" attitude, I had earned a top position (in the top 3%) within our company. I took that opportunity and ran with it.

Eight years later, I am forever grateful to my friend, John. If it wasn't for him closing the door to my opportunity, I may have never opened the doors to countless opportunities. It gave me the opportunity to go after what I wanted and to really dream. Knowing that fear can show its ugly head periodically, I now face those fears head on. I find myself living a life that I control. I am doing things I had never allowed myself to imagine. Owning different companies that were started from an idea and built from scratch would never have been conceivable before. Knowing that network marketing is an amazing way for anyone to succeed allowed me to fulfill my true passion of helping others, not just with my company, but any direct selling company.

Helping others achieve their desires positioned me exactly where I wanted to be, allowing me the same personal interactions I once had with my salon clients. I now experience the joy of life I was so desperately longing for.

TWEETABLE
Fear not...for when you face your fears, your fears may fade. #Christinedirectsales

Christine Brown-Kindred is the co-owner and COO of Cyclone Inspired Products. She has earned a top position with her network marketing company. Christine has a true passion for helping others achieve their goals in network marketing and currently offers coaching. She would encourage you to reach out to her if you have ever thought of entering into network marketing or if you are looking to take your business to the next level.

cycloneinspiredproducts.com
Thesynergysystem01@gmail.com

CHAPTER 17

Overcoming Obstacles Through Resourcefulness and Determination

by Mark Florentino

orn and raised in Manila, Philippines as one of four siblings, I grew up in a tiny, humble home in one of the most impoverished slums in Manila, far from the city lights. We were happy despite the fact that 15 people shared our home. Throughout my childhood, I was blissfully unaware of any disadvantage of my social class, despite having lost my mother to America. One day when I was five, I woke up to find my mother and all of her things gone. She could not bear to say goodbye to me because she knew that it would be a long time before she would see me again. In fact, more than a decade would pass before we would be reunited in California.

I grew up with very limited resources. Even though my mom was sending us money from the US, there were so many of us that she had to support. My grandma raised us including my brothers and cousins. My situation was very unique because even though I lived in the slums, I went to a nice private school. My mom sent me to private school because she really valued education. She did not finish high school and wanted to give me a good chance to be successful in life. I understood my mom's sacrifices and did not waste her resources on frivolous things.

Children are cruel to each other and going to a fancy private school made it worse for me. I remember getting teased in school for wearing old clothes that didn't fit me. I always wore hand me downs, but I grew to six feet and three inches, and I quickly ran out of clothes to inherit from my older brother and cousins. It was okay in elementary, but when I got to high school, people stopped teasing me, which made me feel worse. People pitied me, and that was worse than getting heckled. I decided that I needed to make some money and buy things for myself.

I started a basketball card collection that taught me the beginnings of entrepreneurship. I would make money by educating myself on the value of the different sets of cards and leveraging that knowledge to increase the value of my whole card collection. As my business grew, I was able to buy clothes and was able to blend better with my richer classmates. By the time I graduated high school, I had enough money so that I wasn't asking my grandma anymore for allowance money. Instead of feeling pity for myself when others pitied me, I used the tools that I had and utilized them to the best of my ability.

I always have been very determined to do what I set my mind to. There have been obstacles along the way, but I have always found a way to make things happen. Once I arrived in the US, I found myself joining the US Navy. An example of an obstacle there would be my first duty station assignment. I initially received orders to go to San Diego. Of course, I was so excited. I was living with my family in Los Angeles, and San Diego would not be too far. But, my orders got changed to Lemoore, CA. Lemoore is in central California. At first I hated it, but later I realized that moving to Lemoore was a blessing in disguise. I was able to focus on improving my financial life since there were not a lot of distractions in such a small town.

I have cultivated discipline for as long as I can remember. I may have a little OCD, so maybe that helped with my discipline also. Those years in the military were very structured and instilled organization in my life. From boot camp all the way to when I got out, everything was laid out like an instruction manual that I could follow. That is both a blessing and a curse. I could have stayed in the Navy and just put my life on cruise control. But I had bigger plans. Being in such a structured way of life made me procrastinate on those plans.

While I was in the Navy, I wanted to get my degree in biology. I was almost able to finish it, but the courses required a lot of laboratory time, and my work schedule did not allow me to take those courses which were all scheduled in the morning. That put a wrench in my plans to go to medical school. After six years of my enlistment, I decided to leave the US Navy and join the civilian ranks. When I got out, I felt like I missed an opportunity by not pursuing med school. I then decided to become a nurse. I eventually became a family nurse practitioner. Thinking back, I ended up spending about the same amount of time becoming a family nurse practitioner as I would have if I had trained to become a doctor. In the end, I still became someone that helped people with their health. Again, I used the tools that I had to overcome adversities.

When I went to school to become a nurse practitioner, I used different tools to make me successful. I used every resource that I had to reach my goal at the time which was to become financially independent. I used student loans to help me invest in real estate. What a lot of people don't understand about student loans is that lenders lend more than enough to student borrowers, and that is what gets borrowers into trouble. I hear about newly graduated doctors having 500k in student debt. I was able to borrow 80k and really just used 30k to pay for my school tuition. I used that 50k to invest in real estate. I am not saying to do that, but lenders lend more than enough to pay for school. What you do with the extra is up to you.

My introduction to real estate was the purchase of my first home. This happened in 2005. Looking back, that was a horrible time to buy real estate (as everyone now knows!). I was only 21 years old at the time, and more than three quarters of my salary went to my mortgage. I was terrified that I bought the house, but I knew that it was something that I had to overcome because I did not want to ever be kicked out from where I lived. My family had always rented rooms and apartments, and we would constantly move. I bought it for 215k. It appreciated all the way up to 250k after a couple years and then crashed all the way down to 100k! I did the right thing and kept paying the mortgage. A lot of people just walked away from their homes that were upside down. I understood that my house had lost half its value, but I thought to myself, why would I leave my house to go rent somebody else's house and pay about the same amount of money? That didn't make sense at all, and I was glad I didn't do it. I did what I had to do, which was to pay my mortgage obligation and not blame others. I lived with the consequences of my decision to buy a house until things turned around. When they did, it was greatly to my benefit! To this day, I still have this house, and it is my best cash flowing rental!

Being a veteran gave me access to VA home loans. These were types of loans that were guaranteed by the VA so that a veteran does not have to put down 20% to buy their home. This is a benefit that has greatly advanced my financial independence. For most people, the biggest barrier to entry to homeownership is the required down payment. Not having to save up for that down payment made it a little easier for me to start my real estate investing journey. This is another example of a tool that I utilized to the best of my ability.

As I educated myself further regarding real estate investing, more opportunities opened up for me. Not just in investing, but also in other parts of my life including my health and my personal relationships. I lost 20 pounds by following business principles! I have met people that are truly amazing not just in their craft but also as human beings. I have never met so many millionaires who are very unassuming and humble.

A lot of entrepreneurs are not just good at making money but they also give back a lot. Their passion to help less fortunate people has greatly influenced me. I have traveled to more countries since I began my entrepreneurship journey than I did when I was in the Navy. The world has become my oyster, and I enjoy every second of it. I have met entrepreneurs all over the world, and it has been very interesting to listen to their humble beginnings. Every single one of them had obstacles that they had to go through, figure out, and then come out stronger as a result of making it to the other side. Their perseverance is something that I have seen in myself that has helped me since I was a kid buying and selling basketball cards and making things happen with the tools that were available to me.

My desires from the past were mostly materialistic. As I grew older and was able to afford most things that I wanted, I still felt a void inside me. This really bothered me because nothing I was doing was making me happy and content. I finally figured out that I am made to do better and greater things and to affect people positively. I am determined to help my community through my businesses. My rental properties are all within the vicinity of my neighborhood. Hopefully, when I become more successful, I can help more people, especially seniors. I am expanding my business into starting an assisted living facility within my existing rental portfolio. As my assisted living business grows, I will be looking into providing assistance to senior Veterans that have more limited financial resources.

My desire is to help people. I like helping people in different ways. I am a family nurse practitioner, and I help people with primary care prevention and wellness. I also try to help people by providing homes through my real estate business and providing financial education to my friends and family. There were lots of trials and tribulations, and I learned a lot from all these experiences. Following my passion to help people in turn greatly improved my overall well-being. Use the tools that you have, don't concentrate on the tools you don't have, and you will achieve everything that you have ever imagined, even in your wildest dreams.

TWEETABLE

Use the tools that you have and don't concentrate on tools that you don't have.

Mark Florentino has been a full-time entrepreneur and real estate investor since 2016. He owns properties in California and North Carolina and is expanding his business to include residential assisted living homes. Mark is also a part-time family nurse practitioner working in rural primary care clinics. His wife, Analisa, is a nurse case manager working at a children's hospital. They enjoy finding opportunistic real estate and business deals when they travel across the US and abroad continually expanding their network. If you would like more information, please contact them at www.PassiveIncome.Rent or mtfenterprises@icloud.com.

CHAPTER 18

How a Multi-Million Dollar Entrepreneur Overcame Bone-Crushing Social Anxiety and Fear of Failure

by Jon Correll

I was the kid who shied away from crowds and stayed at home figuring out how gadgets and gizmos work. At 13, I was writing software and creating cool products for the Apple II. It was 1979. There was no internet, no online marketplace. To make money, I would have to make calls and sell. I struggled. It was so hard to put myself out there.

I was only 13, so I assumed everyone would reject me. Fear gripped me, choking the life out of my dreams of doing something great. I was so afraid that I quit trying after the first rejection.

It felt like I was the only one on the planet who had these kinds of fears. Social anxiety and introversion aren't always obvious in others. It always looked easier for everyone else to be successful. I was the weirdo.

At 17, I got a job as a programmer and MIS manager at a government contractor. Sounds impressive, right? Well, it was pure nepotism. My brother got me the job. I was just a pimple-faced teen that taught himself to program in his bedroom. They hired me because I was good and willing to work hard for minimum wage. It didn't take long before I was coding software at my job that was good enough to sell to Fortune 1000 companies.

It all started to come together. I had a direction and a plan. I had cool products. The market was hungry and in need of a real solution—my solution. I could almost taste massive success.

One problem: I related to computers, not people. And I'd have to sell to people! As the possibilities to succeed grew, so did the Great Dragon of Fear. I had many sleepless nights just thinking of trying to sell to people.

Why even try to build products if I can't sell them? Why build a business, when I am destined to fail? Every time I started, the flames of fear swept over me and through me. Nobody had any clue this was going on inside of me. It all seemed hopeless.

What if I try it and everything comes crashing down? And I totally fail. What then?

I feared both trying and NOT trying. I feared failure and success. Some people are "self-made." I was "self-stuck." I had something transformative to offer the market, but I couldn't get out of my own way. So much for impressing the ladies with my tech-savvy selling finesse.

Then one day, I read *Think and Grow Rich*, and the idea of fanning your desires into a white-hot flame was emblazoned on my heart, my mind, and my soul. I had to get around my fears: *Dad tried his hand at entrepreneurship, and failed. So will I. I have a curse that is seared into my DNA. I will fail.*

Fear was an excuse and a lie, and I was fed up with destroying myself and my hard work. I was sick of being mediocre. I had had it. *I must choose to battle my fears or live in failure.* I made a radical decision: I would choose to fight fear with desire. The Great Dragon of Desire was born!

And now it was time—time to talk to PEOPLE.

I had a list of all the Fortune 1000 companies that could use my software. I had to call these industry titans, but...

What if they answer? What do I say? What if they reject me? What if I really am not good enough?

I grabbed the phone and my jittery fingers dialed. The first call answered, and of course, it was a gruff, old, salty executive having a bad day. My voice trembled as I muttered my horrendous pitch. He didn't even understand why I was calling.

He yelled right into my ear, "Don't waste my time kid!" CLICK. REJECTION. FAILURE! So much for desire. I felt the Great Dragon of Fear come back: scaly, menacing, and roaring with fiery laughter. *You really are a worthless piece of...*

I sat there staring at the list of 1000 people I had to call, thumbing through the pages as if looking at them would make things all better. It didn't. The task felt impossible, insurmountable. I was overwhelmed, stressed-out, and lost in my own mind. I was paralyzed by fear.

But then I looked at my written statements and goals, and one stuck out: "I am determined to do anything and everything ethical and good to achieve my goals." *Really? Anything Jon? Even sales calls to people?!*

I grabbed the phone again and kept calling. I had to. One rejection after the other:

- Call 2: "Nope!"

- Call 3: "Stop calling!"

- Call 4: "I'm going to report you. Where'd you get my number?!"

- Call 27: "Who do you think you are?!"

Each call was the same. It was as if I had been called on a great adventure designed to be as difficult as possible. It even felt like these people were notified beforehand to give me an especially hard time. No one cut me any slack.

I decided, *I AM NOT GOING TO QUIT!* I was determined to go through the whole list, even if they ALL rejected me. I turned each "NO!" into "Next!" My desire to succeed started becoming stronger than the many fears holding me back. *I'm not going to be a quitter this time!*

Again, I picked up the phone. The dial tone seemed to blare for an hour in my ear. (Thank you, 1985 phone technology!) My fingers *still* shook. My stomach *still* churned. I slowly pushed the buttons. RING.... RING.... *Please don't answer. Please don't pick up.* RING. "Hello? Hello?"

"Um, uh. Hi, I'm Jon, and I have software that fixes this problem you're having on your systems. Would you like to buy it?"

"What does it do? How much does it cost?" My eyes shot wide open. After five minutes of clumsy conversation, I CLOSED MY FIRST DEAL EVER! BAM!

The excitement of actually overcoming my fears and pushing through was incredible. I fell to my knees from the rush of success and the exhaustion of fighting those fears. I was laughing on the floor like a fool, but at least I was a victorious fool. It felt good. REALLY good. I continued pushing through day after day, getting better and more confident as my skills grew.

Many may read this and point out that this whole battle was just made up in my head. It's true. It really was just in my head. And it was REALLY in there. If you've ever felt even a little fear or trepidation, you know what I'm talking about. I know now I'm not the only one, and I'm no longer pushing through this just for me. I'm pushing through this for EVERYONE that struggles with fear and doubt. We're in this together.

I'd like to say that sale was my last battle with fear, and everything after that was easy, rainbows, kittens, and ice cream dreams, but that's not really how this adventure of life works.

The battles come and go, but it's different. I'm different. Now I KNOW I am capable and can fight through the challenges before me. Even though I can't seem to eliminate the fears completely, I can brave my way through them. I know that NOW. It's NOT about being fearless, it's all about fearing-less through braving more.

Thirty years later, I had an opportunity to sell a new software solution to a billion-dollar client. It was a big deal for me and my software company, one that could be worth millions.

So, I flew across the country to the meeting by myself, equipped with nothing but a pen and a notepad. It was SUPPOSED to be a simple preliminary meeting with the CEO and director of marketing. Easy.

I showed up to their offices thinking I was ready for our "little chat." However, after I arrived, security ushered me towards a very large conference room. *Gulp.* I realized they had planned something VERY different.

I walked into the room, and there sat the entire executive team: CEO, marketing director, CTO, CFO, CMO, COO, C3PO, and a bunch more C's. Over a dozen of them. Apparently, the casual "beer and chips" meeting between the director of marketing, the CEO, and myself was not to be. It had turned into an all-out, everything is on the line meeting to make THE decision NOW. This was, to use a business technical term, a holy $*#^ moment.

As everyone was introducing themselves, another uninvited guest showed up (unwanted and unannounced): the nerdy 13-year-old kid in full fear mode ready to screw EVERYTHING up and prove that I was still a failure after all this time.

Here I was, the CEO of a successful tech company, and I just started freaking out inside.

As the introductions were just finishing up, the director of marketing turned to me and asked if everything was okay. "Sure. Good, good."

Then, the CEO blurted out, "Okay stupid loser of a kid, we're ready for your lousy presentation. Go!" He didn't say the *stupid kid* or *lousy* part, but that's what it felt like.

I went completely blank. "Awkward" would be the polite way of describing me at that moment. The picture-them-in-their-underwear trick doesn't work when your face is pasty as glue and your bald head is as bright as a baboon's butt.

It wasn't pretty. It wasn't fun. My entire head was blaring like there was a five-alarm fire. *Not good.* (Even now, as I write this, I feel a bit embarrassed to share this with you.)

My brain was zig-zagging. My heart was thrashing. *Presentation? I don't have a stinking presentation! This was supposed to be a simple chat! I was told we're just hanging out and having a couple of beers!*

All their eyes were glaring at me, their arms were crossed and there wasn't even one friendly smile in the room.

You're going to fail. You always fail. You'll never be good enough. The lies poured in one after the other into my mind. *Just utter a word, a joke, anything. JUST SAY SOMETHING!*

I did my best "big boy" impression: "Listen, I had about a gallon of sweet tea this morning and looking around the room I may be in for a bumpy ride. I really don't want to spring a leak on your fine furniture. Could someone point me to the nearest little boy's room?" Everyone gave an uncomfortable chuckle, and I left.

I went to the bathroom and stood there looking in the mirror, shaking my head. I stayed close enough to the toilet just in case I threw up. I had flown across the country and all my employees were counting on me. The stakes were high, and I felt the full weight of this burden on my shoulders.

I washed my face with cold water. I took a deep breath and gave myself a pep talk (a bit of a rebuke). *Wait a minute! I am enough. I know what I'm doing. Have some courage, dude! I can do this presentation without slides, with my eyes closed, doing a handstand.*

I said a simple prayer. *God, give me courage and confidence.* I did a quick "shaky dance," thumped my chest a few times, and headed back to the den of lions, head up, shoulders back.

I took my seat and looked around the room. Years of discipline and determination led me to this point. I KNEW what I was capable of. I knew my stuff. *I am what they need. I got this. If they say "No," I will say, "Next." I will just give my best, and that's enough.* A deep sense of confidence and peace filled me.

I gave the presentation of my life. No slides. Lots of questions, many challenges, a couple of rough moments, but I KILLED it! It actually felt… effortless. I was in the flow. The room full of potential haters and fighters turned into fast friends and collaborators. As we began to leave, the CEO said, "That was the weirdest and best presentation I've ever seen. I'm looking forward to working with you and your team personally on this project." BAM!

After more than three decades of entrepreneurship, I've learned that courage and consistent action are the keys to facing and overcoming fears. Decide to let go of the lies and hold on to the truth. Create the desire to push through any pain, any hell. Have the determination to do what is necessary at any moment. And consistently build the discipline to get up and try again DAILY no matter how many times you fail.

You will become a better version of YOU, the person the world needs you to be. You will be able to share your gift so others may learn, grow, and receive the new possibilities in their life they didn't even know existed. You will be confident in your own skin and feel happy to be there.

What fears are holding you back today? It's your time to shine now. You can decide today to live in white-hot desire, eagle-eyed determination, and steadfast discipline. The world needs you!

TWEETABLE

Courage and consistent action are the keys to overcoming fears. Create the desire to push through any pain. Have the determination to do what is necessary at any moment. Consistently build the discipline to get up when you fail and try again DAILY.

Jon Correll is CEO, partner, and founder of more than a dozen multi-million dollar companies with 100's of employees. Having sold his companies, Jon is an active investor, and also coaches and consults with entrepreneurs and CEOs to grow their businesses using custom growth strategies; he has helped 100's of companies over 30 years. He is passionate about empowering entrepreneurs to overcome fears, addictions, and stresses, and feelings of deep overwhelm to get the excitement of building their dreams again.

Are you stuck? Reach out to me personally:
Text me directly: 858-999-8031
Email: Jon@CEOVoodoo.com
LinkedIn: www.linkedin.com/in/joncorrell
Twitter: @CEOVoodoo
Schedule a free Strategy Session:
www.CEOVoodoo.com

CHAPTER 19

You *Can* Have It All

by Gabriel Hamel

"Whatever the mind can conceive and believe, it can achieve."

– Napoleon Hill

You can do anything you put your mind to. My mom told me this from a young age, and it sunk in subconsciously until it became a mantra. I believe this with my whole heart and have proved it in my life. When I was a toddler, I wore leg braces. The doctor told my parents I would never do anything athletic, but quickly I was busting out of my crib. I played various sports as a child and had true success in high school wrestling. I learned that how strongly you believe in yourself directly affects your success. Despite a broken collarbone and a poor record the previous year, I became a state champion wrestler my senior year. An underdog with many doubting me, I won my title through relentless determination and discipline. I had no doubt in my mind I would win.

As I found my success in sports, I began searching for success in business. I grew up in a lower-middle class home with two working parents. Sometimes struggling financially, and often hearing words like "We just can't afford that" or "You can't have it all," I decided to take the only job I knew available to a 12-year-old—paperboy. In sixth grade I was also selling candy bars out of my locker, and in ninth grade it was condoms, though the school shut that venture down pretty quick.

My senior year of high school I joined an Army National Guard Infantry unit that trained on the weekends each month. After graduating, I took on several low paying jobs and even took a few classes at the local community college. I finished reading Robert Kiyosaki's *Rich Dad Poor Dad* as it was becoming crystal clear in my mind that neither college nor working for someone else the rest of my life was the path for me. Not too long after finishing this book, I received the phone call that I was being deployed to Iraq, and five days later, I was gone. While deployed, I thought about the lessons I learned from this book often, lessons in financial freedom through real estate investing. Often ridiculed for saving every dollar I made while deployed, I was determined to come home and buy my first house. I now had a new desire to learn and a newfound determination to be financially free through real estate. For the first time, I was excited to study and to learn.

Jim Rohn said it best: "Formal education will make you a living; self-education will make you a fortune."

After returning home from Iraq, I did purchase my first house. I rented two of the three rooms out to cover my mortgage and started looking for a job. Realizing once again that I wanted to be my own boss and take my financial life into my own hands, I purchased a couple properties over the next couple of years and partnered with a friend to open up a small nutrition store with the little money we saved during our deployment to Iraq. The store never made a lot of money, and eventually my partner wanted out of the business. I lived a pretty frugal life at the time and only had myself to take care of, so I decided to buy his half of the business and see if I couldn't increase revenue.

Since customers were far and few between, I spent most of my time behind the counter self-educating, studying real estate, finances, and business. During this time, my passion for real estate grew, my focus for wealth grew, and I set a goal for myself to be financially free from a job before ever having children one day. I also decided that dating would only distract me from this focus, but sometimes life provides us gifts and brings people into our lives when we are not looking. That was exactly when a young woman crossed my path that I just had to meet. She is now my wife. We were falling for each other fast, and our relationship was moving quickly. We were spending every day together, and it wasn't long before she moved in with me.

One day, I was sitting behind the counter at my store when the realization set in that this business wouldn't provide enough long-term or even short-term income to live on. Even a low-paying job would pay more. I realized that although my couple rental properties produced a small amount of cash flow each month, this too wouldn't provide even a living wage. So, as I was sitting there considering the direction of my financial future and six months into a new relationship, I got a call from my girlfriend that she was pregnant. This was not either one of our plans at this point in our lives. She was also on the journey of fulfilling her own goals and dreams.

My future flashed in front of me. I was only starting to get to know this woman. I was still trying to figure out what I was doing with my life. This was not part of the plan I had, not yet anyway! I freaked. All of a sudden, I felt this pressure to provide for a family and my soon-to-be child.

After many months trying to keep the store financially afloat, and out of concern to provide, I shut the store down, and spent the next several months picking up work where I could, from making phone calls collecting data, to landscaping, to answering help wanted ads on Craigslist. Eventually, I landed an entry level job in a special education class. Though this job provided a great service to these kids who needed help, this was not my calling, and a few months into this job with a one-year-old at home, as I was cleaning human feces that a student decided it would be fun to throw everywhere in the bathroom stall, I started thinking about my goals. Would I continue down a path of a "normal job" because I was afraid to fully commit to my dream of financial freedom? I spent every day reflecting on my ideal life and realizing that for me to accomplish anything in life I must fully submit to the idea once again that anything I put my mind to was possible. So with determination and obsessive-like vigor, I went looking for an investment property that spit off enough income to replace my job. Cash flow became my new obsession, and between telling everyone I knew, passing out business cards, knocking on doors, making phone calls, and scouring Craigslist every day, I finally found a property that would do just this. I wasn't yet rich, but I felt the first taste of financial freedom and quit my job.

Almost all my time and energy was now devoted to building and growing a real estate portfolio. I was singularly focused on this one area of my life, building wealth. Alyssa was working, going to school, and up all night nursing our son. We started spending more of our time together arguing than we did enjoying each others' company. Soon, we were expecting our second son. I stayed headstrong on my financial growth, but my relationship with Alyssa continued to suffer.

Our family was growing, and I was about to close on our new home. Concerned about missing out on even a day of potential rent, I had already moved us out of our current home so I could get a jump on getting the old house ready and start collecting rent. The closing of the new property kept getting delayed and eventually fell apart all together. I now had a very pregnant girlfriend in nursing school, a two-year-old, and no home of our own to live in. Graciously, we had family take us in over the next four and a half months. I realized I had only been focused on financial growth, and growth in other areas of my life were lacking. Even so, two weeks before our second son was born and two weeks before Alyssa graduated nursing school, I had moved us into a new house, and I was back to my ways of chasing my financial goals.

As I continued pursuing my financial endeavors over the next couple of years, my relationship with Alyssa continued to suffer. Only after she picked up and left did I wake up to realize how much I was losing. This became my real wake up call. I had to split my time with the kids and spent many days and nights sitting alone in my empty house and wondering where my life was headed. It was only after I stopped feeling sorry for myself that I started to reflect on my life in more depth. What was actually most important to me? What was it that I actually wanted out of life? I realized that it wasn't only wealth that I was after but also happiness, my health, and close family connection. I had created in my mind this self-limiting belief that you had to choose one over the other. At one point I had even blamed Alyssa for my lack of happiness and for standing in the way of my financial goals. I realized that my growth had only been in financial growth, and of course it had, that's where my time and energy was spent. I realized that though my real estate portfolio had grown, I wasn't growing as a person. I wasn't who I wanted to be. I wasn't the best version of myself. So much of my time and energy had been spent on becoming a successful real estate investor, but I had studied nothing on personal development, happiness, relationships, marriage, or parenting. Nothing!

For me to grow as a whole person, it was imperative that I studied personal growth. As I started focusing my time and energy on personal growth and becoming the best version of myself, every area of my life improved. Alyssa and I rebuilt our relationship into something beautiful and more amazing then we ever thought possible, and we now support each other every day towards growth. I spent time studying relationships and parenting and became a better parent to my kids and a better listener to my family and friends. I spent more time and energy on my health and fitness goals, and I am healthier today than I have been at any other time in my life. Subsequently, as my focus went away from the money and towards improving myself, my real estate business also had massive growth.

I'm here to tell you, you can have it all. Ignore the naysayers in your life. These people don't own your dream. They don't get to decide how your life turns out. You do! Focus your time and energy on the things that are truly important to you.

For me, it's personal development, family, health, wealth, and happiness, and they are all intertwined. I strongly believe that being healthy, wealthy, and happy are choices, and with the right knowledge, and more importantly, effective action, these states can all be greatly achieved.

Happiness is not something that we can let others control, give, or take away from us. Happiness is the practice of gratitude, the ability to see the good in people, and the ability to not fall victim to our circumstances. Life can bring to us many great obstacles and people filled with hate or negativity. Ultimately, we must be accountable for our actions, for our reactions, and for our own happiness.

Jim Rohn eloquently said: "Happiness is not something you postpone for the future; it is something you design for the present."

TWEETABLE

You can do anything you put your mind to. Don't let self-limiting beliefs decide the life you live. Focus your time and energy on becoming the best version of yourself. Your results will be a byproduct of your thoughts and actions.

Gabriel Hamel is a real estate investor who values time-freedom, health, wealth, happiness, and family. He focuses his time and energy learning, living, and growing in these areas with his wife and two sons. Gabriel strongly believes that health, wealth, and happiness are choices, and with the right knowledge, and effective action, they can all be greatly achieved.

Connect with Gabriel at
Gabriel@Hamelinvestments.com
Instagram: Gabrielrhamel
Facebook: Gabriel Hamel

CHAPTER 20

From High School Dropout to a Six-Figure Income (Part-Time)

by Tracy Davis

B e warned, after reading the following principles you will no longer have excuses for why you don't have everything in life that you wish to have. If you're not where you want to be in life, if you ever thought you were capable of achieving more, then I just want to encourage you to incorporate the following principles that you are about to read into your daily life. All the knowledge in the world is useless unless we incorporate and apply it into our daily living. Thank God, finally at the age of 50, somebody showed me these principles and I started to apply them to my life.

Before I knew about these principles, I guess you could say I was a thug, or at least I made many poor decisions. I drank to the point of passing out, got into drugs, robbed people, and dropped out of school. My cousins were not even allowed to be around me without adult supervision. I spent some time in juvenile hall. I was headed down the wrong path. I saw some of my friends going to jail, saw some of them shot and killed, and many of them just becoming bums. One day I took a look at my life and realized that if I didn't want to be a bum or land in prison, I had better do something. So, I joined the Army. Well, I wasn't ready for the Army. The next three years I never really excelled, but at least I received an honorable discharge.

For the next 20 years, I went from job to job. I would quit a job right before they were going to fire me. I got married and had two wonderful children who deserved way more than I could give them. I got divorced then remarried, then divorced and remarried the same woman four times. Are you kidding me? Talk about not learning from your mistakes. How many people would marry and divorce the same woman four times? Boy, was I confused. Finally, I went to work for the Oklahoma Department of Corrections, not because I wanted to but because I had to. I thought it was my last, best chance to be successful. I also joined the Oklahoma National Guard. So, for the next 20 years I bought into the 40, 40, 40 plan. You know the one: go to school, get a good job, go to work for 40 years, work 40 hours a week...then retire on 40% of what we can't make it on now? Does anybody really still believe in this system the way I did?

While in the Army, deployed to Kuwait, I met this little old, frail, Kuwaiti man named Othie. We started talking, and I asked him his story. I loved listening to him talk. Othie just had a way about him. He was sure of himself, but not cocky. He seemed like he just wanted to share some of his life lessons. I bought him lunch and must have listened to him for an hour. All of a sudden, he stopped, looked at me dead in the eyes and said, "Only when we start searching for our dreams, only when we take action and begin pursuing what we truly desire, will we be truly fulfilled. Until then, we will always feel like something is missing." I was speechless. Where did that come from? I felt like something was amiss all my life. What was this old guy talking about?

Before I could say anything, Othie asked me if I was playing to win the game. I said, "What do you mean?"

He said, "The game of life, son. Are you playing to win the game of life?" I sat there for a second, and after thinking about it, I realized I was so busy just trying to get by every day that I wasn't playing to win the game. How could I win the game when I sat on the sidelines for the first two quarters? Othie kept talking, he said, "For most of our lives we seek opportunities, and it seems we want them presented on a silver platter. We just need to recognize great opportunities don't show up on a silver platter, they show up disguised as problems. When faced with a problem, most of us only see the problem; we never see the opportunity. It's only when we start to block out the problems and look for the opportunities that our life will begin to change." Again, I was speechless. How did this old man have all this wisdom?

Othie said, "I want to encourage you to look for the opportunities in every problem and play to win the game. The difference between successful people and unsuccessful people is that successful people make a conscious decision to play to win, and they have a time perspective. Time perspective is the amount of time that goes into planning our day to day activities. If we are in the game, we may as well win! Winning all boils down to this—if our subconscious blueprint for success is not set, nothing we do, know, or learn will ever make much of a difference."

WOW, this old crazy man was blowing my mind, but I intuitively knew he was right. I had to get back to work. I asked Othie if I could meet him at the same coffee shop tomorrow at the same time if I agreed to buy him lunch again. Othie gave me that big ol' smile and said, "Sure thing." The next day, I couldn't wait to get to the coffee shop, and he was there waiting on me. He greeted me with that smile of his and invited me to sit.

I said, "Hey Othie, how you been?"

Before I even got the words out, he said, "If you want more out of life, I have good news. You have just completed the first step. The first step is just wanting more. It's just having the desire to become more, desire to give more, the desire and determination to achieve more. It's no secret all it takes is desire and determination." He must have seen the puzzled look on my face because he then kept talking and said, "Everybody is born with the same endless opportunities, potential, abilities, hopes, and dreams. Some people strive to live up to their potential then quit when they perceive it to be too hard. Some people deem it too hard and never strive at all. A few, a very few, realize that all it takes is an extra 1% effort applied daily. That extra 1% of effort, plus a burning desire and hard work, is all it takes. That's it, nothing more. It doesn't matter what side of the tracks you're born on. Your religion doesn't matter. Your sex, age, current circumstance, or past don't matter. The past is the past. All that matters is that you have a burning desire for success and are willing to apply the extra 1% effort that it takes in order to achieve the success you desire. Once that is realized, there is nothing holding you back." Who was this guy? He was amazing. It was like he had all the answers. Where in the heck did he come from? Othie asked, "Are you happy with your life? Are you living out your dreams?"

I said, "Yes, Othie, I'm happy. I'm not sure about living out my dreams. I'm not sure anybody is really living out their dreams."

Othie looked at me with disgust and shouted, "Have you not heard anything I have said?" He said, "You can accept mediocrity, or you can achieve your dreams. THE CHOICE IS YOURS. All it takes is that extra 1% effort and the burning desire I spoke of." Othie said, "I have to go—I just want to encourage you, the next time an opportunity crosses your path, take it. You seize the opportunity and apply the extra 1% effort, and soon you will be living out your dreams." I too had to return to work, so we agreed to meet there again the next day.

That night I received a message from one of my Soldiers that had been hurt and sent back to the Wounded Warrior Project. He spoke of a business opportunity. Now, this soldier had spoken of many opportunities in the past, but the timing was not right, my attitude was not right, my blueprint was not right. This time, after talking with Othie, I was taking advantage of this opportunity. It was a network marketing opportunity. I knew nothing about network marketing, but I knew I desired MORE out of life. I knew I had a DREAM, and I knew I could apply 1% more effort. So, I took the opportunity, and I was excited. I decided that if other people were successful, why not me? Why not now? All I needed to do was be willing to follow what successful people were already doing and be willing to outwork everybody.

The next day, I raced back to the coffee shop to tell Othie about the opportunity. He was nowhere to be found. I asked the people who worked in the shop if they had seen him. They didn't know who I was talking about. I described him, and they said they had never seen him. I nearly shouted, "The guy I was speaking with for the last two days!" The guy at the counter said, "Sir, you were in here alone the past couple days. We didn't see anybody." I stood there dumbfounded. I thought somebody must be playing a joke on me.

Anyhow, the information was powerful, and I was going to apply it.

The next two months I learned as much as I could about my new business and looked for Othie every day. The day came when we were going back home to the United States. I never did find Othie. When I returned home, I would go back to work at the Oklahoma Department of Corrections, but I would also work on my fortune part-time in my new network marketing business. As soon as I returned home, I developed a schedule of when I would work my part-time business. When I saw my dad, he said there was something different about me. Dad said I seemed more purposeful, like I was on a mission, like I was driven. I explained about the revelation and the conversation I had in Kuwait with Othie.

Dad asked me to describe him, so I started to describe him, and as I did, I saw a puzzled look that I had never seen before appear on my father's face. He said, "Wait here." He left and went into the other room. I heard him throwing things around. When he came out of the room he was holding a picture. He showed me the picture and asked me if I had seen it before. I was speechless. It was Othie.

I said, "Where did you get a picture of Othie?"

Dad sat there and started to weep. He said, "This is a picture of your great grandfather." I looked at the picture again in amazement. Was I dreaming the whole thing? Did he come to me in a dream? The employee at the coffee shop said there was nobody there. Had my great grandfather really spoken to me? Either way, I wasn't going to focus on this, only on the principles he taught me. And I went to work on my dreams and goals.

I have to admit, when I talked about what I was doing with my friends at work, I had most of them laugh at me, but every day, no matter how tired I was after work, I would go out and build my business. After five months of working my business, I was making over $20,000 a month part-time. That's when I told my beautiful wife Jodi that she didn't need to work anymore.

I continued to work my full-time job because I liked the PART-TIME story. After another five months of working full-time in the Department of Corrections and part-time in my network marketing business, my part-time income continued to explode. Eventually, it just didn't make any sense for me to keep working at the Department of Corrections, so I walked away from my full-time job. The last six years, we have helped countless people earn a six-figure income and hundreds of people make an extra thousand dollars a month, all working part-time.

These principles helped me step out of a life of mediocrity and into a life where I fulfilled all my dreams and desires. The second year after I began applying these principles, we were making close to $500,000 a year. Wow, what a difference a year makes. Today Jodi and I have it all: lifestyle, money, friends, a great marriage, an unbelievable spiritual life, and most of all, freedom and opportunity to teach others how simple it is to achieve massive success. Today, I'm proud to say I have several six-figure earners in our organization. My biggest fulfillment comes from teaching people how to generate money from home, but it wasn't always this way.

Until Othie taught me that it was okay to dream again, and that all I really needed to do was apply an extra 1% effort, I was like a ship without a rudder. Today, I offer money back guaranteed mentoring. It's not about the money. It's about showing others how easy it is. It's about showing others how to win the game of life. If a high school dropout, knuckle-dragging prison guard can be successful, anybody can be successful by applying the right principles.

TWEETABLE

We don't need some magic skill set to be successful. I know plenty of skillful people who are homeless. If we want to win the game called life, all it takes is a burning desire, a little discipline, and 1% additional effort.

Tracy Davis is an international speaker, bestselling author, and life coach. He is a disabled retired Veteran of two combat deployments. He is currently writing another bestseller. Tracy is a top 5% earner in the entire MLM industry. He was a unit manager at a maximum-security prison and earned a master's degree at the University of Oklahoma. Today, Tracy and his wife Jodi enjoy teaching others how to create six-figure incomes working from home. In fact, Tracy gives a 90 minute free consultation teaching how to maximize results. 405-623-4076. All speaking engagement fees go to homeless Veterans. He can also be reached at tracy@ineedzeal.com

CHAPTER 21

A Win for Small Business

Stealing a Page from Private Equity to Build a $22 Million Business

by Rocco Sirizzotti

We wanted to sell.

We really liked the guys and the company that were pursuing us.

We were discussing a $3M valuation!

But then they decided to go another direction and opted out.

We were terribly let down.

We had been growing our company for 15 years and were eager to sell, but now our perfect buyers were gone.

We realized, however, that in telling us their plans for our company post-acquisition, they had shared with us something more valuable than the $3M offer price we would have gotten.

> *"Every adversity, every failure, every heartache carries with it the seed of an equal or greater benefit."*
>
> **– Napoleon Hill,** *Think and Grow Rich*

We had the DESIRE to sell and to maximize the price that we could sell for.

With DETERMINATION, we applied their plan of acquisitions and multiple arbitrage over the next several years to purchase other companies and integrate them into our core business to create tremendous value.

And, our DISCIPLINE was rewarded four years later when we sold for $25M versus the $3M we were originally offered. It was an 8x increase that turned our major let down into a huge win for me, my partner, and our long-term staff.

Heather Stonner and I owned and operated Medical Logistic Solutions, Inc., a medical courier business based out of Denver, Colorado. Starting with 9 drivers in 1994, we grew to over 500 employees doing $22M in annual revenue with daily deliveries across 27 states. It was no overnight success (20 years, in fact), but we learned and implemented some things in the last few years that significantly accelerated our growth and allowed us to achieve an 8x increase in our sale value.

What we learned is not something new that we developed (very few ideas in this world are truly new). But it is something not often known by small business owners like us. Instead, what we learned and implemented are strategies used repeatedly by private equity firms to quickly build value. Private equity has a well-oiled system that seeks out solid, mid-sized companies with good systems then implements these strategies to multiply values and sell companies for big gains. By implementing these strategies, we were the beneficiaries of significantly increased value before we sold.

Heather and I felt like we stumbled upon these strategies through good fortune. We were approached by some hard-working, ethical buyers from a Fortune 1000 company, who utilized these same successful strategies to grow their company to $1B+ in revenue. They wanted to add a new division of medical courier services to their company that would sit alongside their medical waste disposal services. When they eventually made the decision NOT to pursue acquiring us, we were very disappointed. But these guys had already shared with us the plan of how they intended to grow us from $5M in annual revenue to $100M!

One of our common sayings at Medical Logistics was "**Time to put our boots on,**" which we used whenever a situation required just getting in there and doing it. Heather and I applied this core belief and sought out the right people to help us implement the plan ourselves. Through some business friends, we found and partnered with Jeff Lovill and Craig Zoellner who brought their experience with mergers and acquisitions. We structured an agreement that "**put us all on the same side of the table**" wherein they only benefited when we benefited, and together, we set out to rapidly grow the business.

Over the next four years, we had an exhilarating run, growing revenue 4x from $5M to $22M, but more importantly, growing the value of the company from $3M to a final exit price of $25M for an 8x increase in value. AND we had achieved my long-standing goal of becoming one of the leading medical-specific courier services in the country in terms of revenue, employee drivers, and geographical coverage area! Not bad for the son of blue-collar immigrant Italian parents.

For the first 15 years of operating our business, Heather and I grew the company like most small businesses do: incrementally, one customer at a time, striving to provide great service at good value and then asking for more of their business.

Large companies and private equity firms, on the other hand, grow their companies via acquisition. Why?

Benefits of acquisition:

- Quickly add top line sales revenue

- Grow geographically

- Add talented key staff with each acquisition

- Potentially access technology, systems, infrastructure, new customer niches, and knowledge of how to service them from the target company

- Gain relationships with national clients to cross market to their existing geography

- Increase efficiency and decrease overhead costs as a percentage of revenue by increasing size

But the best reason is "multiple arbitrage."

Understanding Multiple Arbitrage

In our industry, like many others, the value of the company is based on a multiple of revenues or earnings. The larger and more stable a company is, the larger their earnings presumably, but also, the larger the multiple applied to earnings to determine value. Smaller courier services (less than $1M annual sales) sell for a multiple of 1-2x EBITDA (Earnings Before Interest, Taxes, Depreciation, and Amortization, or essentially, the net profits). Mid-sized companies ($1-10M annual sales) sell for 3-5x EBITDA, and larger, more stable companies sell for 6-12x EBITDA.

Using the benefits of multiple arbitrage to maximize our future exit value, we applied one of our core beliefs, which is **Crawl, Walk, Run**.

Crawl: With what we learned, we now knew that future buyers would be valuing us based on our earnings, and so we spent a year improving our systems and processes and streamlined our costs to improve our bottom line.

Walk: Then we bought the operations of four out of five of our franchisees. These acquisitions were easy because they mostly operated under our model, company brand, and logo, already. So, integrating them into our base operations only required bringing their drivers under our employ.

Run: We began to buy other medical-specific courier companies. We reached out to over 100 couriers that we thought had some focus on medical. In the end, we made four acquisitions of outside courier companies.

Trax Courier in Portland, Maine provided us a foothold in the northeast.

Custom Couriers which operated throughout Wisconsin also expanded our geographic service area but, even more, expanded our service offerings to dairy milk testing labs.

Action Couriers serviced Idaho and Utah plus had a core competency in servicing pharmaceutical wholesalers which we leveraged to land a big contract in Colorado two years later.

ECS Couriers of northern Colorado strengthened our relationship with hospital networks.

So, using our knowledge of multiple arbitrage, we bought several small operations at 1x annual net cash flow, which is a fair price for that size. From our discussions with our Fortune 1000 buyer, we were calculating our valuation at 5x earnings. So, adding the profits we just bought at 1x the small company's annual earnings to our larger and more stable company's bottom line increased our value 5x versus what we paid for the smaller acquisition. We would literally quintuple the value of what we had just purchased in a short period of time with the economics of multiple arbitrage.

And the pattern continued as we grew. The purchase price of our acquisitions of outside couriers were typically at 3x their earnings. Because of our growth through acquisition, our eventual exit was valued at 8x our earnings. So, our investment in these mid-sized couriers nearly tripled in value through multiple arbitrage.

Debt:

With our strong balance sheet, our partner Craig was able to secure a loan facility that provided 100% loan to value on an unlimited number of acquisitions so long as we bought at a 3x multiple or less. But the loans required that I personally guaranteed them. So, $7.2M in total acquisitions translated into $7.2M of loans that I was signed on.

That was a big deal for me. It was a little scary. We had always had very little debt on our balance sheet. This debt had the potential to wipe out my entire net worth.

That highlights another of our core beliefs: **Be Bold. Pull the trigger!** When you need to act, don't wait until your back is against the wall. The universe rewards action over inaction.

Factors that increased our likelihood of success with acquisitions:

1. We narrowly defined our target market (medical couriers) and bought only those couriers with a similar focus.

2. We had strong processes. Franchising our model earlier forced us to create and implement best practices across all geographic divisions.

3. We proactively beefed up technology systems (ops, accounting, HR) to support rapid growth.

4. We had strong and incentivized key staff to implement our decision for rapid growth. (I extended equity to my top six key staff members which I am proud to say resulted in my paying out $5M in bonuses when we sold.)

5. We had a strong balance sheet to secure acquisition financing.

6. We owned very few vehicles but instead compensated drivers for using their own vehicles. Low asset model equals low capital requirements for growth.

7. We **Pulled the Trigger.** We had the risk tolerance to double down.

8. We were in an industry where most of the market is made up of small operators allowing us to pool the smaller players to form a national platform.

9. We were in a growth industry (medical).

Key goals that increased a smooth transition after we purchased:

1. Do NOT lose any customers of the acquired company. Losing a customer reduces the top line sales revenue and, more importantly, significantly erodes the net profits on which we valued the acquired company.

2. Retain ALL the key staff of the acquired company. This seems counter to what we usually see in an acquisition. Typically, the buyer immediately slashes the staff of the acquired company to cut costs. Instead, we felt that every employee has a certain amount of "**tribal knowledge**" that was important to retaining customers.

3. Integrate the operations of the acquired company with your company. We kept both names for a while. We weaved our logo and colors with that of the acquired companies. We placed new employees onto our HR platform and migrated customers to our online order and dispatching software.

4. Review the best practices of the new company for ideas and processes to roll out to the rest of the company.

5. Maintain consistent, clear communication. Communication is the key. Rumors of the sale spread quickly, so we decided it was better for us to communicate during the acquisition rather than letting the fear mongers do it for us. On the first day, we announced the purchase and introduced ourselves in person to all employees that were available. We had an announcement email prewritten which we then sent to all employees, customers, and vendors. I personally called the decision makers of every key client and set up a face to face meeting within the first 30 days.

6. Promote the benefits of the merger. We promoted our intention to keep ALL the staff to build a larger more stable company, we often offered better benefits for the employees, better technology, plus more efficient systems and professional processes, and we extended the geographical reach and service offerings to customers greater than the smaller companies we acquired were able to offer.

7. Don't get started too late. Maximizing your exit value in the final sprint may take three to five years. We had four buyers come and go. Each one was an exhausting dog and pony show culminating in a letdown. You need energy and passion to get through it. Those five years for me were an exhausting, but also an exhilarating time. Maximum value comes when you are on a growth trajectory, not when sales have flattened or are declining. All that takes energy. It takes discipline and determination.

And as a final thought: There are times when I think I would have liked to stay in longer and take the time to double again the size of the company. But as a business owner, I knew that I didn't get to decide WHEN to exit the business. It's the buyer's decision when and what to buy. But with desire, determination, and discipline, Heather and I created the environment that made our business attractive. We grew to an attractive size. We had a proven model and systems that would survive our departure. We had growth on a steep trajectory and showed that the organization was capable of handling rapid growth and integrating future acquisitions. In short, we maximized our exit value. Thank you, Heather and the whole Medical Logistics team!

Today, Heather and I own and operate a real estate investment, syndication, and property management company in which we pool our funds with other investors to purchase, rehab, and manage investments in multifamily, land development, and income-producing agriculture.

"For no matter what we achieve, if we don't spend the vast majority of our time with people we love and respect, we cannot possibly have a great life."

– Jim Collins, *Good to Great*

TWEETABLE
Be Bold. Pull the trigger! When you need to act, don't wait until your back is against the wall. The universe rewards action over inaction.

Rocco Sirizzotti is a small business entrepreneur and member of the Austin, Texas chapter of Entrepreneurs Organization (EO). Passionate about small business, he volunteers as a mentor and coaches small business owners to double down and use acquisition and multiple arbitrage strategies to maximize their company values prior to their exit. In addition, he speaks about his own growth and exit experience.

Rocco also writes a newsletter which vets alternative investments in small business and real estate. Current projects include multi-family apartments, a portfolio of single-family rentals, land development for custom homes, farm investing, and hard money lending. Subscribe to his monthly investment newsletter at GratefulInvestmentGroup.com

CHAPTER 22

It's Not Over, I Am Just Beginning

by Keisha Brooks

'll never forget the sound of the vault being closed as we laid my father officially in his resting place. It was like the sound of a mine worker banging a metal hammer to concrete. The clanging noise was so electrifying, I could feel every nerve of my body throb to the sound, and I then knew that it was done. He truly was gone.

The day I received the call, it had been three weeks since I had given birth to my third child with my husband. I was standing on our front porch waiting for my mother to exit her vehicle when my phone rang. The news came from my aunt, his sister, and as she began to tell me what had happened, all I could do was fold over. Luckily, my mother was there.

The next few weeks would feel like the longest days of my life as we waited for the body to arrive back to the States from Haiti where he had been visiting. The wait felt like forever while we planned and made arrangements with the embassy just to get our father, husband, brother, cousin, and friend back in our possession so we could properly lay him to rest. That night, after the flood of sadness that overwhelmed me, I felt as if his spirit were with me, as if he wanted to reach out and touch me but knew that would break some mortal law. I am not quite sure of the transition that takes place from when a person dies to when they arrive to their eternal place, but I do believe my father's spirit was waiting for the right moment to ascend. The whole time from the grave site, to the gathering at the reception hall, to traveling back to the house felt like a whirlwind. I just wanted to wake up from the horrible emptiness because on that day a part of me was buried with the man I once called Dad.

In that moment, all I could think about was the memories. Memories of living together before my parents divorce. Memories of the reason my parents divorced in the first place. The emotional, financial, spiritual, and physical abuse that occurred as a result of being raised by both Christian and Muslim customs with no guide of what agreement or alignment could be. Memories of standing in our kitchen and my father telling me that I was going to be a millionaire one day. Being told of this man everybody else knew, valedictorian, top of his class, leader, influential mentor of his community, versus the guy I knew, a stern father working three jobs, providing the best for his family, an entrepreneur, a fisherman. Fast forward to being taken on a train away from the only place I knew as home, the East coast, to the Midwest. To a house that I didn't care to be in. To a place of just Black and White from the multiculturalism I knew.

I'll never forget when we first moved to the Midwest. I was now considered what was known as the minority, and it showed in the classroom and the neighborhood. I didn't even know that I could be considered a minority. It was as if my eyes were looking through a different lens of the world. I still didn't like the thought of being taken away from what I knew as my home and many times considered suicide as an alternative.

The benefit of moving was being able to have a fresh start. Change can be good and bad. You just have to decide which side of it you want to be on.

"Worrying about something you can't change will forever be the biggest waste of your time."

– unknown

So, I made new friends and tried new things such as basketball, choir, track and field, and debate. With both track and debate I did well. It was debate where I discovered my desire to be a lawyer. By the time I graduated from high school, I had very few friends, but I felt like I had achieved that milestone of earning a diploma for myself and no one else. During this time, I took time to reflect and recalled memories of my father providing simple life lessons, like ask good questions and speak up when you are talking and want to be heard. I didn't realize it then, but I was already starting to build a brand for myself by making sure I was educated and taking care of my physical and mental well-being.

I also was growing more spiritually, and during this time, I fully committed to being a young Christian woman. I didn't feel as if I had to choose between Muslim and Christian, but I took the opportunity to discover my own outlook on Christianity, as not just the religion. I had never felt like I could fully discover Keisha. I wanted to test other ways to express myself, but really I was just becoming brave enough to be myself. And so, I was determined to lead and not follow because I noticed following led to depression, sickness, and loneliness, which was what I did not want.

Knowing who you are and having the desire to share that as well as the discipline to push through the process of performing at such an elite level takes guts. The world will give you a reputation if you allow people to. You must be centered and confident enough to eradicate the bad stereotypes.

By this time, I had finally met my husband. Right from the start, our attraction was mutual. I wasn't even thinking about dating anyone, mainly because I had finally started back in school studying to be a forensic scientist. I was infatuated with science, but I also loved to analyze and research information. I was determined to pay for my schooling, so to start, I worked two jobs and went to community college. Let's just say I slept on the days that I had the fewest classes.

They say everything is intentional when it comes to your journey. I intentionally wanted to date someone long-distance because I was focused on finishing my degree. I also wanted to be sure that any relationship I pursued was going to be *the* relationship. I didn't want to waste any time. And wonderfully, I got a military man.

"Life is a series of natural and spontaneous changes. Don't resist them; that only creates sorrow. Let reality be reality. Let things flow naturally forward in whatever way they like."

– Lao Tzu

In the long run, I wanted to pursue law and be a lawyer after earning my forensic science degree. However, I fell in love with this strong, ambitious, good-looking guy. Justin was different from the start, such a gentleman and over achiever. As time went on, I personally knew that for me to be the woman that I desired to be, I had to change my mindset. I did so by journaling. I had a few different journals, one for my big dreams and another for short-term goals, such as my health and well-being. I also had a journal where I just wrote poetry. I used to just love putting words to rhythm. I even thought at one point that I would be a famous poet like Maya Angelou.

I knew I wanted to be famous not just for the attention but to be able to share my story with many other young women desiring a happier lifestyle. I wanted them not to feel like their looks were what was going to get them the right guy or the right position. You know how they say you always want to make your parents proud? It wasn't that for me. I simply wanted to make myself proud.

When you go through hardship, it takes a form of mental toughness to be successful. Throughout my life, I have dealt with being emotionally unstable, and it could be because of my upbringing. When two individuals are never aligned, it can cause a certain type of turmoil or chaos from within, and I was the type of person that never exposed myself. I've always had a brick wall, a lack of trust for others. It took all of me to open up and trust my husband from the start.

When I think about it, it has taken all of me to fully trust myself with the potential that I have to help others. After the death of my father, I once again was emotionally unstable. You would think that is typical for a person who is grieving, but I felt like mine was a little deeper because it brought back memories good and bad, and it took me a year and a half to truly get from underneath the dark cloud and grow into my full potential of being a wife, mother, and entrepreneur. I couldn't even function in the role I had at that time as a "support" to my husband and our real estate business. I started to wonder if I was I truly satisfied with being a person who was in real estate. For a while, I thought that I was being of good value to my husband by supporting his idea of entrepreneurship. But that wasn't enough because we were becoming stagnant and not growing or excelling like we needed to in the business and even within our marriage. I realized that what was missing was deeper than just support. Having a partnership was the way to make us whole. When you think about life partners, you think about growing old together and having a family, but establishing a partnership is much more. It is about building a legacy.

The turning point was realizing that I didn't want to fall victim to a generational curse but rather create a generation of victory. I wanted to be the one to shift my family tree. And then we read *The 5 Love Languages* by Gary Chapman. Learning to speak one another's love language is what my husband and I lacked, and what our parents never portrayed before us. My father always told me to do better than he did. I had thought that meant academically. I realize now that it was more than just in one area of my life. My parents were divorced, and I didn't want that. He wanted me to do better than he did in every part of my life that is of value and that brings value to others.

My grandfather owned hundreds of properties, and my dad was a businessman and entrepreneur. My mother is a seamstress. I wanted not only to emulate their success, but also to spread that success into generations of my family to come. It is great to have a gift, but if you are not sharing that gift with the world you not only short yourself, you waste good talent. So many individuals desire to do something different, like retire early, but they lack the ability to grow within their gift and end up growing within someone else's.

One day at a time, I had to find discipline for myself and do better for me. Paying attention to your inner self takes time to practice and accomplish. I even had to develop self-worth in my relationship with my husband. At one point, it seemed as if we were on slightly different paths, both achieving goals but not the same common goal. The death of my father truly made me think about the life that I have. My father was an individual that did not allow his condition to limit him from fulfilling his goals and dreams.

For me, quitting is never an option. Today, inspired by my father, I dare myself to do different every day in my life and my business. I inspire others now with my partner and husband Justin Brooks as an investor, speaker, and podcast host. Together, we invest in real estate property and operate a real estate investment fund that manages a multimillion-dollar portfolio which specializes in developing assisted living homes. Our podcast *Real Life Real Equity* is the platform we use to teach other entrepreneurs not only how to better their wealth, but also their life and wellbeing as entrepreneurs and business owners. We highlight our success and the success of other entrepreneurs across the nation. It's not over. I am just beginning as the extraordinary woman I am, doing extraordinary things for my legacy.

TWEETABLE
Don't allow your condition to limit you from traveling to your destination. With grief comes peace.
www.realliferealequity.com

Keisha Brooks is a Boston native, wife, mother, podcaster, real estate investor, and coach. She is an alumni of Columbia College. With her discipline of criminalistics, she has learned to analyze and research "in between the lines" of business deals. She also helps listeners grow their worth with her podcast Real Life Real Equity with her husband Justin Brooks. Keisha is also an inspiring fitness coach. She has been able to help individuals see self-value to better every area of their life. To contact, email keisha@realliferealequity.com and follow on Instagram @marietheentrepreneurswife

CHAPTER 23

Desire

How a Small-Town Kid with Bad Eyes Became a Fighter Pilot

by John Haney

"Your eyes are fine, you're just never going to be an Air Force Fighter Pilot."

The words hit me like a brick wall. A punch in the gut. How could this possibly be? Becoming a fighter pilot was the ONLY thing I wanted to do since I was a little kid. When I voiced this concern aloud, the nurse simply looked at me and laughed. That began my adventure to prove people wrong and live the life that I wanted to live, regardless of what other people said was possible.

Growing up in a small town teaches you a lot about life. My town was driven by agriculture and small business. I learned a lot about hard work and commitment as a kid working odd jobs. I cut grass, worked at a pharmacy and a hospital in the summer, raked leaves in the fall, and shoveled snow in the winter. I got involved in lots of extracurriculars in school (sports, show choir, and theater) not because I was particularly good at any of them, but because the barriers to entry were low. Those experiences taught me a lot about life and about myself. They gave me the courage and confidence to dream big and believe that anything was possible. Ultimately, they put me on the path I needed to realize my dream of becoming an Air Force Fighter Pilot.

My first task was to get into college. Initially, I thought about attending The Ohio State University, but that was out since I couldn't get a scholarship to go there and didn't have enough money to pay my own way. Next, I looked at Wright State, but again, I couldn't pay the bills. Finally, a family friend said I should check out the US Air Force Academy. Everyone that went there got a full-ride scholarship. No tuition fees. What a deal! I quickly found out I wasn't the only one with the bright idea to attend the Academy. Turns out, it was pretty competitive. So, what's a guy to do? I worked as hard as I could inside the classroom and out. I loaded up my schedule and learned a ton about time management, a skill that would be crucial to my success in the future. Through hard work, some solid relationships, and a bit of luck, I was able to sneak into the class of 2006 at the Academy.

Life at the Academy was a drastic change. Having no background or experience with the military, I quickly learned that things weren't quite as happy go lucky as the movie *Top Gun* made them seem. Days were filled with rigorous physical military training and academics. The system was structured so that you always had 30+ hours of tasks per day but only 24 hours to complete them. At first, this overload was maddening. I was used to getting everything done on time and just right. There was no longer enough time for that. Looking back, this was one of the formative learning experiences in my life. The hustle and bustle and ultra-competitive atmosphere taught me to prioritize that which is most important and forget the rest. It forced me to choose where I would focus my energy and spend my time. If something wasn't a worthwhile project, it would get tossed to the side and revisited when time allowed. This stress enabled me to figure out what was truly important and give it the attention it deserved while forgetting about the things that weren't as important and saving them for times that I had more resources to take care of them. My biggest realization at the Academy was that there are a LOT of people that are FAR more intelligent and talented than me. By the end of high school, I had a bit of the "big fish small pond" syndrome, thinking a bit too highly of myself. College woke me up to the harsh reality that, despite what my mother told me as a child, I was nothing special.

As soon as that sunk in, I had a choice to make. Would I sit there and sulk, upset that in a sea of overachievers I was well below average? Or would I make up for my lack of brains with my incredibly strong work ethic and will power that were forged in my small-town upbringing?

I pressed ahead and vowed that I'd work as hard as I could, as long as I could, and try to keep up with the smartest kid in each of my classes. Finding the rockstar of each course wasn't hard, but keeping up with them was. I soon realized that there are some people in this world that are simply gifted, able to look at or hear something once and remember it perfectly from then on. Having somehow missed this skill in the proverbial gene pool, I doubled down on efforts to improve my study skills. By focusing on how to study properly, I improved my standing in class. I was never the top of the class, but I was almost always in the top half. Using that strategy, I finished my time at the Academy in the top 10%. Not bad for a kid from middle of nowhere Ohio.

Before leaving college, we had a series of briefings to help prepare us for what lay ahead in our careers as Air Force Officers. While most of the messages were forgettable, our Commandant of Cadets said something that stuck with me to this day. She said, "Success is where preparation meets opportunity."

Going to pilot training, I applied the lessons I learned at the Academy. Once again, I was surrounded by people far superior to me. On the first day of training, everyone in the class talked about themselves and shared what they wanted to fly. In my class of 33, more than two thirds wanted to fly fighters. Problem was, we were only going to have three fighters for the entire class. Again, I found the sharpest person and did everything I could to keep up with them. Unlike some things in life where you have multiple attempts to get things right, flight school was a once in a lifetime opportunity. This was my opportunity. To be successful and achieve my lifelong goal, I needed to be prepared. There were no do overs, no opportunities for a second chance.

This was a test. What kind of person was I? Would I rise to the challenge? All you can do is your best. That I knew. I also knew that if I didn't give it everything I had, I would always look back and regret it. That thought was the motivation I needed to push myself and work harder than I ever had in my life.

My attitude was epitomized by the quote painted on the floor of the 336th Fighter Squadron in North Carolina that says, "Today I do what others won't so tomorrow I do what others can't."

I had 54 weeks to realize my childhood dream or wonder "what if?" for the rest of my life. So, I took my opportunity. I ate, breathed, and dreamed flying. I learned the airplane's systems inside and out. When others were relaxing, watching movies, or having a beer at the bar after a long week of 12-hour workdays, I was devouring aircraft manuals and mentally rehearsing the proper execution of maneuvers. I became obsessed. Putting in the extra hours was the only way I was going to be able to best the others in the class who had much more experience and were far better pilots than me. That commitment to preparation made all the difference.

Becoming the best requires that you give everything you've got day in and day out. I hit bumps in the road and experienced setbacks daily. Everyone does. No one has ever flown the perfect flight. That said, I realized you have to keep pressing forward and putting in the work. Sooner or later, you will get noticed and that hard work will pay off. The question is, are you willing to work hard enough and long enough to get noticed? That's what separates people that talk about doing something big and those that actually achieve something big.

During pilot training, it was apparent that becoming a fighter pilot entails much more than just being able to fly a jet. Having decent hands and being able to make the aircraft do exactly what you want when you want is important, but sound decision making is also important. Even more important is your willingness to be a team player. What makes a fighter squadron such an incredible place is not just the aircraft parked on the ramp, but also the camaraderie that its members share. It's the ultimate fraternity. This is not lost on the leadership in pilot training. They are evaluating every student not only on their flying skills and ability to regurgitate procedures flawlessly, but also their willingness to help their fellow students in the ultra-competitive training environment. By helping their classmates out, they may be giving them an advantage, but they do it because it is the right thing to do. It's the same thing in life. By giving to others, you may lose a little bit in the transaction, but in the end, you typically come out ahead. This was a big lesson for me. Life doesn't have to be a zero-sum game where one side wins and one loses. By giving to others and helping them out, you can both win. Taking this lesson to heart, I made a point of helping out my classmates anytime the opportunity arose. It wasn't always convenient, but it always proved fulfilling.

In the end, assignment night came and went. I got my fighter. Thanks to the countless hours of preparation, I seized the opportunity presented to me in pilot training and achieved my lifelong dream. It was an incredibly gratifying experience that paved the way for my future successes.

After more than a decade of flying fighters for the US Air Force, I'm transitioning to my next stage of life. In recent years, I've become a real estate investor, focusing on achieving solid returns for my fellow investors and improving the lives and communities we invest in. I carry the lessons the Air Force taught me about courage, preparation, and commitment and apply them to my investing. My next adventure involves improving the lives of families living in low income housing and helping them rise above their economic hardships to achieve a more prosperous future. Some people might say it can't be done, but they might also say a kid with imperfect eyes can't be a fighter pilot. I will prove them wrong and continue living the life I'm meant to live, making the world a better place along the way.

TWEETABLE

Success is where preparation meets opportunity.

John Haney is a former Air Force Fighter Pilot with three combat tours and more than a decade of fighter aviation experience. He is also the founder of Open Skies Investments, where he invests in single and multifamily real estate, as well as international agricultural opportunities. He is expanding into low income housing opportunities to improve the quality of life for people in those communities and offer them greater opportunities for a more prosperous future. If you want to learn more or become a part of his journey, you can email him at crane.haney@gmail.com, check out his website www.openskiesinvestments.com, or message him on LinkedIn. He currently lives in Tulsa, Oklahoma, with his wife and two kiddos.

CHAPTER 24
Farm to Failing to Fantastic
A Lesson Learned

by Darren Seys

I moved from the farm in Moline, Illinois, home of John Deere, and ten years later I would end up with a struggling ad agency in glamorous Boca Raton, Florida. That is, we were struggling, until I went to a conference and one speaker said one thing that changed everything.

The year was 1988. I graduated high school the year before and was broke, living and working on the family farm and as a stock boy at Walgreens. I opted to move to Daytona Beach with the concept that if I was broke, at least I could be broke on a beach. It's there where I met the art director for NASCAR International Speedway Corporation, Jerry. He drove a black and gold 1988 Trans Am GTA, and I thought, *Wow, he is who I want to be!*

Growing up, I was always into art, as were my two brothers who were actually better than I was. So, I visited Jerry's little office just off of turn four at Daytona International Speedway where he worked with one other person. I said, "If that guy ever leaves, call me."

Well, a couple of months later, he did leave, and Jerry invited me over for an interview. He told me to "bring my portfolio." I had no idea what a portfolio was let alone what it would contain. I arrived anyway. We had a great time chatting, and Jerry took a risk on me. There, working in the shadow of the 31 degree banks of turn four at the most famous NASCAR track, I began my graphic design career which ultimately laid the foundation for starting my own ad agency in Boca Raton!

I started Peak Seven in 1999 and enjoyed some early success until September 11, 2001. That day the world changed, and with the majority of my business in aviation, it hit the agency hard. As a young entrepreneur, I thought it could not ever get that bad again.

I survived, only to have the real estate and financial markets crash in 2008. So, there I was with 70% of my business gone in a matter of days and unable to collect on hundreds of thousands in receivables. The economy was in a tailspin with no light at the end of the tunnel. I was terrified! I just had my second child, and the amount of stress I dealt with each day was overwhelming. I had too much pride to not honor my obligations to printers, media outlets, and many other creditors. I was using my credit cards to pay other credit cards all the while paying for a credit line at the bank. To make matters worse, the credit line was converted automatically into a term loan which increased my monthly obligation even more. I thought about closing the doors, but I simply could not do it, this is what I loved to do. It was my passion. The agency was ten years old with many employees there since the beginning. Burning through my savings and operating in the red for over a year, I was paralyzed on the next step. *What should I do? How do I change my situation knowing it was literally a matter of months before my juggling of creditors and lack of income would come to an end?*

That's when I joined the Entrepreneurs Organization globally known as EO. I was referred into EO by my client and now friend Dr. Mark Sanna. In the first year of my membership, I was very insecure and felt I did not belong, but I stuck it out knowing I needed business help, I just did not know what help it was. My forum, me and eight other entrepreneurs, would meet each month with a structured EO format. In order to get the full benefit of forum, you have to be open and honest and share your top 5% and bottom 5% of issues.

Each month, a member of the forum would present a challenge, business or personal. I would present how my company was struggling and losing thousands of dollars each month. After a while, I sounded like a broken record, so we did an open and honest brainstorming session to find out why I was in this rut and how I could get out of it. We had yellow sheets of paper everywhere on the walls with notes along with many great ideas. At that meeting, I realized that I simply did not have the right team in place nor did I have the ability alone to achieve my goals.

However, after that meeting, I still did not make any immediate moves, knowing it meant letting go of loyal, long-time employees. My forum was telling me to make moves, the numbers were telling me to make moves now, but it was as if I could not believe I was in this situation. My ego did not help either. I felt I could solve anything, plus I had never been faced with this much adversity. I even considered quitting EO merely to avoid facing my forum mates each month with no action plan. They meant that much to me.

I started to go to all of the speaking events that EO offered, and that is when I ended up at an event with Jack Daly in Fort Lauderdale in 2011. It was about building better sales teams, and how to get more out of people. I sat there listening to Jack's high-energy, in your face speaking style, like I had other speakers, waiting for the one take away I would actually implement in my business. As he scribbled on a flip chart, drawing diagrams for success and yelling how to do this and that, he stopped and asked this question, **"When is the last time one of your employees gave you a good idea?"** As I sat there thinking about it, I realized my employees didn't give me any ideas. Jack then followed up with this impactful statement, the one that changed my outlook and business to this day. **"The fastest way to new ideas is new employees."** BAM, it hit me dead in the face. I got chills as everything my forum had been telling me crystalized at that moment. That was the one thing I needed to hear to give me the courage to make changes.

I knew I needed to change up my team, but now I knew the **WHY...**for new and better ideas! So I went back to my forum and said, "I know what I have to do and more importantly why," and with their help, I systematically rebuilt the agency staff from the ground up. It was, of course, difficult to let employees go that had been with me for so many years, but I had to put the business first. After ten months, I had successfully replaced my entire team with people that had the skills for today's advertising and marketing, and more importantly, brought fresh new ideas and perspective into the agency.

The new team not only brings ideas to the table, but also challenges me. Hell, they actually respectfully argue with me! The company has evolved into a much more dynamic agency since the day Jack asked that question. I learned a lot from this experience, the main lesson being you are only as good as the team you have around you! Now this farm boy from Illinois has a thriving agency in Boca Raton along with a team full of ideas!

In the end, it is not only important to recognize and define your challenge; you must also take action to change or you will just be another broken record. Surrounding yourself with positive and inspirational peers you trust and respect, in my case EO, is key to helping you solve challenges both personally and in business.

"Can anyone remember firing someone too soon? The longest time in a manager's life is the day you lose faith in someone and the day you do something about it."

– Jack Daly, CEO at Professional Sales Coach

TWEETABLE
You are only as good as the team you have around you.

Darren Seys is an entrepreneur, speaker, and founder, CEO, and creative director of Peak Seven Advertising in Boca Raton, Florida since 1999. Darren began as a creative artist and became lead illustrator for auto racing giant NASCAR. From the dot-com era through the real estate explosion, Darren has built and launched successful branding campaigns for some of the world's leading names including Honda, Toyota, Shell Oil, W Hotels, Waldorf Astoria, BE Aerospace, Monterey Boats, Northrop and Johnson, and Lennar Homes.

Email darren@peakseven.com and visit https://peakseven.com/

CHAPTER 25

The Path to Success is Paved With Perseverance

by Dr. Lee Newton

I contemplated the letter that had been sitting on my desk for a few days. I could not bring myself to open it. I knew what it said, and I could envision its content reducing my life to rubble—smoldering ashes and wilted dreams of what might have been.

"It is always darkest just before the day dawneth" (a well-known quote credited to Thomas Fuller) provided a shred of hope. My resolve had all but been extinguished.

When I finally opened the letter, my fear became reality. The bank was formally notifying me that I was in default of the loan on the building that housed my eye care practice. I had made all my payments to them—a couple times late—but I had made every single payment. However, they were citing two other provisions of the loan covenants: I was not current with the property taxes, and a downturn in the real estate market had caused the loan balance to exceed the current asset value.

Those dumb asses, I thought. I had proactively reached out to them over a year ago—anticipating several challenging months—and had conveyed sincere intentions to be accountable and work cooperatively with them. And this was how they responded.

How did I get myself into this mess, I wondered. I had always been successful in everything I had done in life, and now I was on the verge of failure.

My career started on a high note. I graduated optometry school in 2000 and purchased a practice rather than work for someone else. Even then, I had the entrepreneurial spirit of independence. I owned the building where the practice was located, and two years later I purchased the adjacent building to secure additional parking. The practice grew year after year, and things were progressing according to my plan. It was here in my own practice and my own office building that my real estate and construction experience began because early in my career, I could not afford to hire contractors for every project. I did not envision these experiences leading to a second career in real estate development.

Consultants

After a few years of growth, the practice started to plateau, and I perceived that it was limited by a small office building and congested parking area. I hired a consultant to help me determine whether to maximize my existing space or find a new practice location.

I have hired consultants twice in my career. Most successful business owners learn and grow from outside, objective input; I also wanted to learn from others' mistakes before I made too many of my own. The first time was barely a year into my career as I believed it would be beneficial for my staff to hear the same things I was saying from an "expert."

The second time was then, when I felt I was outgrowing my facility. The consultant agreed that I needed a larger facility, and advised me to purchase a building in a better location. It was one that I wasn't sure I could afford.

After soul-searching, I determined it was a manageable risk. I purchased the building in late 2006 and hired a contractor for the renovations as they were well beyond my skill set. My practice build out left me with almost 5,000 square feet of extra rentable space. I estimated 12-18 months to find a tenant. Unfortunately, it took more than four years and consumed nearly all of my personal liquidity. Remember, in the recession of 2008 most businesses were contracting, not expanding. However, the long search for one tenant led to two good tenants...so, I took another leap in 2011 by putting a 4,200 square foot addition on the building to accommodate both. With improved cash flow, I thought refinancing the mortgage and paying for the renovations would be easy. Yet, banks didn't want to talk to me. I did not understand. How did I borrow seven figures in 2006 only to be rejected with stronger cash flow in 2011? Later, I would realize that banks weren't talking to anyone during that time.

With limited hope of securing conventional financing, I decided to pursue a private loan. The consultant had previously pontificated about his successful network of multimillionaire clients, from doctors to businessmen, worth as much as nine figures. When I asked if he had any connections who would be interested in a short-term loan, his response was, "Why did you have to be greedy and rent to both businesses?" That was our last conversation.

I learned that consultants will never know more about your particular business or situation than you do. They may be experts in your industry and may make broad and general recommendations based on their knowledge, but they are not authorities on *your* business or *your* life. You alone are accountable for your decisions.

How Not to Make $1,000,000 in One Day

While under bank scrutiny, everything was difficult. Their distressed assets manager required monthly meetings, during which he would belittle and chastise me. Dealing with him created veritable fire and fury inside me. What was not immediately apparent was that this appalling treatment would fuel my steadfast determination to succeed.

The context of my situation, and of real estate in general in 2010, was recessionary. All property values had gone down. The bank noticed and required an appraisal. The result was a disaster. Because the appraiser had mistakenly characterized a large portion of the property as warehouse rather than finished office space, the value was half of where I needed it to be, and at least $500,000 less than what I owed the bank. I was so furious about this terrible appraisal that I could not see it as the blessing it would be: it maximized the amount by which the bank perceived I was underwater, and they wanted out. Yesterday.

The bank's way of dropping me was by selling my note to a venture capital firm in early 2011, causing things to progress further out of my control. I had worked on the problem for years, tenants were scheduled to move in, and now I faced yet another challenge and a new creditor. How would they handle my situation? Should I disclose that I was in the middle of a construction project, adding 4,200 square feet to the building to accommodate two tenants? These were difficult times and circumstances for which my didactic and clinical training left me unprepared.

Friends asked me, "How do you sleep at night?" But sleeping wasn't a problem, getting out of bed was. My wife would tell me, "I need money for grocery shopping," and all I could think of was the $5,000 I had spent on plumbing fixtures that week. It's easy to look back and conclude that I had been depressed, but it's hard to be objective when you're actively struggling with something. Poor decisions with respect to our health (e.g. eating, sleeping, and exercise) easily become embedded and are tough to change. Self-pity is convenient but may cause one to avoid challenges rather than confront them. I remember concluding that my primary responsibility was taking care of my family. I knew that my loving wife and our two sweet daughters weren't the cause of my difficulties and should not have to suffer due to my business circumstances. I owed them my very best work, every single day. Living Jim Rohn's adage of "you are the average of the five people you spend the most time with," I was careful to associate only with friends possessing the qualities I strived to emulate. I consciously made better decisions, developed the habit of starting my day at 4:30 a.m., and made exercise a daily priority.

I told myself to keep holding on, but my hands were becoming sore from what appeared to be a no-win situation. My new creditor required financials, and I didn't know whether a positive or negative spin would be more beneficial. I even began to wonder what would characterize a favorable solution. I never thought that merely re-introducing the loan proposal to a bank that had previously rejected me could propel me toward success. Since the property had been improved, the improvements mostly paid for, and the new tenants were paying rent, they now felt the deal deserved funding. *How ironic*, I thought. Looking bad on paper is what caused the other bank to dump me, and looking better on paper is what closed this deal. I considered the disclosure required by SEC Rule 156 on an investment offering: "Past performance is not indicative of future results."

My version: *Future success is not predicated on past failures*.

My good fortune continued; I obtained another, better appraisal, and I was able to negotiate a discount on the payoff from the venture capital group. The increase in appraised value plus the loan discount was more than $1,000,000. Despite no increase in tangible assets, I felt as if I had finally succeeded.

As I emerged victorious from the dark cloud that loomed over me for so long, I recalled a phrase uttered by saxophone Professor John Nichol of Central Michigan University. I had confessed that I was nervous, having to open a concert with a saxophone solo in front of 2,000 people back in 1993. "Big moments, little lives," he said to me. My interpretation: *neither our highs nor our lows are as meaningful to others as they are to us*.

The Value of a True Friend

Fred was my architect, my friend, and the vice president of the construction firm handling my building addition. He was highly talented, respected, and accomplished in design and construction. Fred was always correct in his assessment of a situation. One such instance was the December 2010 planning commission meeting. The commission had approved the site plan for my building addition, giving me the green light to expand. "Do you realize what just happened?" he said. "They approved you without any exceptions, conditions, or issues. Things never go this smoothly!"

I replied, "This must have been meant to be."

"Be careful," Fred warned me. "I have other clients trying to finance their projects, and they aren't getting anywhere with banks right now. Lending has really dried up." Of course, Fred was exactly right.

Indeed, after the work was completed in 2011 and the balance of the construction contract was due, I was not in a position to pay. I felt it was important to apprise Fred of my continued efforts, though I had nothing to show for them. "Lee, I never doubted your integrity," he replied. "Keep working and you'll get past this." Months later, during the refinance, the bank sent Fred an email to inquire as to the total amount owed. Fred's reply remains on my bulletin board:

> The total revised contract amount due is $212,017.72. A cashier's check is preferred, and a sworn statement and lien waivers can be provided upon your request. No lien has been placed on the property since we have always had total confidence in Dr. Newton's word.

When I read that email, something became very clear. A true friend is someone who treats you the same whether you owe him over $200,000 or nothing at all.

Fred passed away in the fall of 2018—too early at 70 years of age. His legacy in architecture, building design, and construction will certainly outlive me.

Reflections

Through my academic career including eight years of post-graduate studies, the only financial education I received was what I had the drive to learn on my own.

Like many entrepreneurs, I read Kiyosaki's *Rich Dad, Poor Dad* early in my career—what a refreshing approach to economics. He articulated different views about income/expenses, assets/liabilities, and financial education than what society would have us believe. I realized that in order to be financially independent, I would need more sources of income than an 8-5, Monday through Friday job.

Resourcefulness and multiple sources of income helped me hang on despite adversity. I was so far behind on property taxes that I risked losing the property to tax foreclosure. Fortunately, one of my alternative sources of income, trading options, produced enough revenue to pay the property tax bill. Mainstream financial advice will tell you that options are risky; I agree. Any investment governed by forces beyond one's control is risky without attention to position sizing and asset allocation. Let me tell you what is riskier: following mainstream financial advice of investing with the expectation of capital appreciation rather than for the certainty of cash flow.

My perseverance in completing the renovations during my darkest hours and renting to both commercial tenants provided the cash flow to save my business and real estate. During the process, I also acquired tremendous commercial construction experience. I now own, either personally or with partners, several office buildings and multi-family rentals. I am negotiating with one of the largest banks in Michigan interested in divesting land adjacent to one of my developments. Although weekday office hours remain dedicated to eye care, my experience managing both the investment and construction aspects of projects has attracted other doctors, surgeons, and high net worth individuals interested in partnering on subsequent ventures.

It is said that luck is the confluence of preparation and opportunity. Perhaps a corollary is that the resolution of life's challenges can come from hard work and tenacity along with the desire, discipline, and determination to succeed.

TWEETABLE
Never allow your dreams to be limited by the reality of your present circumstances.

Dr. Lee Newton is an optometrist, real estate developer, and musician. He and his wife, Mollie, have two daughters, Anika and Chloe. Lee has experience as both a general contractor and syndicator; his tenants include billion dollar corporations. Current projects include an office building and a residential housing development. Lee's community involvement includes the founding of an eye care charity, his Rotary membership, serving on the board of directors of McLaren Bay Region Hospital, and serving as chairman of the Downtown Development Authority of Bangor Township, Bay County, Michigan. Contact him at Lee@CEassets.com.

CHAPTER 26

The Breakdown that Got Me to Stop People-Pleasing and Go All-In on My Passions

by Erika De La Cruz

I didn't realize that I was in a state of fight or flight for a little over a year.

I desired a life fulfilled and a life where I could say yes to every single opportunity that came my way. What I didn't foresee was that the body and mind limit our capacity to say yes to everything. Basically, I underestimated the care needed to sustain my well-being. I just assumed my body and mind was a machine and that I should say yes to every opportunity. I kept people-pleasing. I had 99 people to get back to at the end of every day. And yes, I had huge opportunities rolling in.

Basically, every time someone would say jump, I would ask how high. Every time someone would call, I would answer. If they extended me an invitation, I would show up to the event. Because for a while saying yes to opportunities was how I built the success that I had.

What I didn't realize was that you get successful by saying yes to everything, but you stay successful by saying no to almost everything.

One day my body decided to tell my mind that we needed to take a break. I lost the feeling in my hands and my upper facial area for about three months. I didn't understand it until I started talking to other overachievers and naturopathic doctors who said that this was common in a physiological breakdown. My mind thought everything was alright, but my body was screaming:

Put me to sleep! Take care of me! Get me a massage! Start saying no! Take care of yourself!

I couldn't argue with physiology. I clearly couldn't feel my hands or face, so I put my entire world on hold. It was one of the scariest things ever. I stopped my newsletters. I stopped doing the online content that I was participating in. I even told the Hollywood Punch Report, the network that I was working for at the time with Punch TV, that I needed to take a serious break. I went on a retreat with my fiancé and recuperated in Mexico, digital free! I took time to re-evaluate what was important to me, what I was doing to fill space, and I realized that all of my yeses were created because I was afraid of losing what I had built. I was afraid that if I stopped the yeses, the opportunities would stop rolling in.

I realized I **was** doing a *bunch* of things well, but I **wasn't** doing a *few* things exceptionally. I was bombarding my schedule until it was overloaded, and I'm so thankful that my body had a crash course in store for me so that I could learn that lesson.

As hard as it was, I started putting my phone away after 7 p.m., using things like coloring books instead of television, and saying no to even casual dinners or brunches because I needed to preserve time to just get well. I eliminated 90% of what I was doing previously and decided to really concentrate on just the 10% left. It was a beautiful blessing in disguise because it caused me to ask myself what I was truly passionate about. I asked myself, if I had one week to live, what would I devote my time to? What was clear was that only three of maybe a hundred things I was doing, was I truly passionate about. My Passion to Paycheck brand, my online community, and television meant more to me than anything. I doubled down on all of the above and ended up having a sold out Passion to Paycheck event. The Passion to Paycheck brand was picked up by Focus TV network and is now a talk show. I've grown my online community, doubled it! And I'm now the official entertainment reporter for a brand called Average Socialite, something I only dreamt of previously!

I'm not saying it was easy and that I didn't get a lot of blow back. People were upset that I was saying no. People were questioning why I wouldn't take 8 a.m. calls anymore. Instead, I exerted the discipline to make sure that my schedule allowed for absolutely no calls, no lunches, and no meetings before 11 a.m. No electronics after 7 p.m. It wasn't until seven months in that I started to feel like myself again: well rested and getting random compliments from my community saying how fresh I looked. I didn't even realize what bad shape I was in the year before. A lot of the things I started saying no to meant a lot of people were left, well, pretty angry. Eventually, I realized the people who understood and gave me the time to do me, be me, and take care of myself, were the ones that I wanted in my life. I learned that I could show up as me 100% in my truth if I was asking myself the questions: Does this make me happy? Is this exactly what I want to do? Now, I straight up do not do it if the answer is no.

I was determined to experience success in my career **AND** my health and well-being. With discipline, I was able to accomplish that. Incorporating my wellness habits have even led me to expand my digital presence by adding a vlog that's the real Passion to Paycheck experience, documenting not only my day to day life inside of my career, speaking on television and the show, but also my trials and tribulations with sleep health and well-being.

My commitment to a well-balanced life outweighed the costs of people getting angry or me having to restructure my schedule or miss out on late night Instagram posts or television. I can now share my experience with others because I authentically overcame it, and all it took was one year of discipline with my routine and habits, my desire to live a well-balanced life, and my determination to live a life for me instead of others. You can't make everyone happy, but if you start with yourself, you can guarantee that one person will be.

TWEETABLE

You get successful by saying yes to everything, but you stay successful by saying no to almost everything. Know what you are passionate about and take care of your well-being above all else.

Millennial Erika De La Cruz is a media and TV host and personality, red carpet correspondent, and brand ambassador of fashion week San Diego. She works with the CW TV Network, Variety's Night of the Stars, *and NBC. She is the Lessons From Network Millennials Expert, and is the author of the book* Passionistas: Tales, Tips and Tweetables From Women Pursuing Their Dreams. *Her event Passion to Paycheck teaches the ins and outs of the TV hosting world with major guests, and her vlog Passion to Paycheck showcases the true nature of the business.*

CHAPTER 27
Self-Discipline
Your Road Map to Success

by David Wallach

I learned the difference between discipline and self-discipline the hard way.

My parents got divorced when I was 10 years old. They immigrated to Israel from Romania following the Holocaust. My father came from an Orthodox Jewish family and mom came from a non-religious family. My brother and I were born in Israel. Since my brother is almost 11 years older than me, he was able to choose where he wanted to live when they divorced. Of course, at age 10, no one asked me for my preference. Living with my dad was a constant challenge because of his orthodox upbringing and his wish for me to follow an Orthodox Jewish education and lifestyle with a modern neighborhood, school, and friends. From age 14 until I graduated high school at age 18, you could say I was a rebel. I resisted every bit of discipline he tried to impose on me. The '70s were before the computer games era. I went straight from school to the playground to visit friends, anything other than stay home or study. School was a social gathering for me. I felt no need to achieve good marks. I just did the minimum to pass. Graduation in Israel means your next chapter is joining the Israel Defense Forces to live the soldier life for the next three years or more if you decide that is a lifestyle that you like.

When I graduated, I was recruited to the very prestigious Pilots Course, and I felt like I was already in heaven as soon as I got the official notice. So there I was, 18 years old, Mr. "No One Can Tell Me What to Do." Wrong! The Army has a very unique way of (and an important task in) dealing with guys like I was in 1978.

First, you meet your Sergeant. You are still confident. Then you make your introduction to your platoon's Staff-Sergeant. Once you meet him, your confidence starts getting a little shaky. The next six months transformed me and my platoon friends into disciplined soldiers. During basic training first flights, navigating, and writing exams at 1:00 a.m. after an entire day of training and being sent to sleep by your Sergeant at 11:00 p.m., the Sergeant and Staff-Sergeant became our gods. When they said jump, we just jumped. When they commanded "Drop to the ground," we hit the ground before they finished their command.

Discipline was instilled in us via sleepless nights and night and day exercises and drills. We became self-disciplined personally and disciplined as a Platoon. All of the guys were trying to do their best, and more importantly, we started supporting and helping each other. We became a unit, not just a platoon of soldiers.

Being 6'4", I was supposed to be a Navigator and not a Pilot. (That being said, I will never forget the experience of flying a Super Cab 150.) Six months into the course, I decided I didn't want to be a Navigator, and I joined the infantry. The six months I spent in the aviation course, the self-discipline that was instilled in me by our Sergeant, Staff-Sergeant, and Officers were invaluable in how the rest of my Army service developed. I realized that discipline and self-discipline save lives! Very quickly, I became a Radio & Communication Platoon Staff-Sergeant. I had to be the one making sure every soldier knew what their job was and how to do it, as well as make sure we had every piece of equipment working. Most importantly, I had to instill discipline in them so they would be able to safely go back to their families. I learned (and later forgot or ignored) two big lessons from my time serving. First, the best way to lead people, whether in the Army or in business, is to lead by example. Don't ask others to do what you are not willing to do. Secondly, "shortcuts are written in blood." Stay disciplined. Follow the road. Don't try to cut corners or it is not going to end nicely.

A few years went by, and my wife and I were married with our first born. I worked in the insurance industry, but, my desire was always to own my own business. With a partner, I decided to start an insurance brokerage. We took the time to explore office rents and labor costs for admin personnel, negotiate with different insurance companies' terms and conditions, prepare potential prospects for the day we would be open for business, and shop for the best office furniture deal. Eight months of preparation and negotiations ended with us opening our insurance brokerage April 1990.

Within a few short years, I realized my desire to own a business was still there, however I had no passion for being an insurance broker or even to stay in the industry. It was 1994, 13 years after I left the Army. Did I remember self-discipline? Did I remember the rules of "Shortcuts are written in blood," or "Lead by example?" Of course not, I just wanted out of the insurance industry. Here is the rule of thumb. If you want out of something, anything, you have to maintain self-discipline to the highest standards and execute self-discipline during the entire process of exploring how to change your course of life.

Guess what I learned the hard way: lack of self-discipline hurts the people closest to me—my wife, and by 1997, our three kids. I wanted out of the insurance industry right away. First, I sold my portfolio, which was an excellent, balanced, profitable portfolio. It sold within 48 hours, and as part of the sale, I had handcuffs for a year. I had to work at the office of the insurance broker that bought the portfolio. It was pure torture. I wasn't only doing what I already hated, once again my desire to be the owner was not fulfilled and I had a new Staff-Sergeant giving me orders. *Someone get me out of here, please.*

Our next-door neighbor and friend was looking to open a new business venture. He knew I wanted out and asked me whether I would partner with him. My reply was the beginning of my problems. I told him, "Whatever you find, let's do it." My self-discipline was out the door. Ignoring the rule of no shortcuts, I was looking for the shortest and fastest shortcut available.

He found a small business for sale, which marketed and produced cleaning supplies, an industry and type of work I had no clue about. "Let's buy it. We can do it better than the current owners. We don't need to do a thorough due diligence. It is very simple. We can handle it."

Since I had already owned and sold a business, I could have taken the lead and said, "Wait a minute. We need to go deep into due diligence since both of us have no clue about this market or industry." Never mind that, I just wanted out of insurance. This was the biggest mistake of my life, a mistake that cost us a lot of money and friendships, caused unnecessary stress to the family, and left a mark on each and every one of us. This was a lesson in how lack of self-discipline can cause you disaster.

Fast forward. We live in Canada now. In 2014, with a partner, I launched Triumph Real Estate Investment Fund. We raise money from the public, from friends, and from family and acquire commercial real estate in Canada and the USA. Now, discipline and self-discipline are the foundation of my due diligence process. Each and every property we acquire, and especially those properties we decide not to purchase, are the result of our disciplined due diligence process. This time, I personally walk every property, climb on each roof, and meet and interview as many tenants as possible. I visit each commercial bay or office. I interview and hire professionals to conduct building assessment and environmental reports. I have a team of real estate professionals reading and analyzing each lease, and I hire mortgage brokers to get us the best financing available. I have lawyers, real estate agents, and property managers in each market we are active in. Above all,

I built a board of professional people to ask me questions, challenge my decisions, and approve or reject my recommendations to acquire a property or dispose of assets.

The reason I walk every property, climb every roof, check the HVAC systems, and talk to tenants is simple. Now that I am responsible for hundreds of investors and millions of dollars, I follow the two fundamental rules of self-discipline. First, "Shortcuts are written in blood." There are no shortcuts in our due diligence process. Second, "Lead by example." When your investors, brokers, real estate agents, and all team members see your commitment to the process, they trust you and will follow your lead to form a solid, professional team that is able to find great investments for your investors.

There is no substitute for self-discipline! It is always hard to keep it. However, it is necessary to avoid costly mistakes. The short-term pain you must endure following self-discipline will be replaced with long-term success, joy, and profits.

TWEETABLE
The short-term pain of self-discipline you must endure will be replaced with long-term success, joy, and profits.

David Wallach is founder of Triumph Real Estate Investment Fund, supplying investors opportunities in North American commercial real estate, and owner of Barclay Street Real Estate, a commercial real estate brokerage in Alberta, Canada. David chairs the Calgary Economic Development Real Estate Advisory Committee and is a cabinet member raising funds for Calgary's neonatal units. He volunteers with the Israeli Wounded Soldier Organization and has been a board member of TCN Worldwide for the past six years. Before immigrating to Canada, he served as GM/president of a professional basketball team. With his zest for life and sense of humor, David interviews entrepreneurs and business coaches on his radio talk show Taking Care of Business.

Connect with David on LinkedIn, Twitter, and Instagram, and listen to his weekly talk show: www.voiceamerica.com/variety, www.triumphref.com, dwallach@triumphref.com

CHAPTER 28

Doing Good, Despite Not Doing Well

Failing in My Health Care Business

by Brian Boyle PT, DPT

With one last bang of the gavel, the judge's decision was final. It was officially over. Or I wanted it to be anyway. No one had told me it could end like this. A decade earlier I would have never imagined that everything I had worked so hard to build would suddenly come crashing down like a typhoon claiming its spoils and washing them out to sea. How did I end up here?

You see, there's a saying in private practice health care which states, "In order to do good, you have to do well." Meaning, if you want to be able to do good deeds and help people in your practice, your practice has to do well enough to stay in business. Perhaps no one in health care understood this notion more than Dr. Hunter "Patch" Adams.

Dr. Adams, the physician and clown, best known because of the 1998 film *Patch Adams* starring Robin Williams, needed additional funding for his practice to continue to do the good work he was trying to do for free. After 12 years of trying to make his practice work, Dr. Adams decided to go public and make a name for himself to draw awareness and financial backing to his cause. He knew he needed to do well, just as I did. But what about those who can't make it? It's not a stretch to say you aren't doing well as a physical therapy business owner if you are standing in front of a bankruptcy judge.

I've always felt fortunate in that I knew what I wanted to be from the age of 17. My strong desire to help and to give back to others would ultimately lead me to choose a career in health care. That and the fact that I really wanted to work with athletes, but am squeamish of blood, made me figure pursuing physical therapy was my best choice.

By most standards, I considered myself successful. I earned my Eagle Scout at the age of 15. I was a two sport varsity athlete in high school and college and an accomplished long-distance runner. I managed to get through a bachelor's and then master's degree program in physical therapy in five years and at the age of 22 was working in my chosen field. I would then pursue and obtain my doctorate, thus achieving the highest degree in my profession. Everything I had really wanted and worked for, I had achieved. I guess I was naive enough to believe that with desire, a little hard work, and time I could be successful at anything.

Up until that point in my career, I had defined myself as both a physical therapist and as a business owner. It was who I was and as much a part of me as was my own skin. Now what? How would I define myself? Who was I? It was then I learned defining yourself or your self-worth by your business or profession, while tempting, is acting short-sighted in a long-term game.

I was reminded of a conversation I had with the late Darryl Dawkins, aka "Chocolate Thunder," NBA Basketball legend, and at the time, coach for the USBL Valley Dawgs. I had asked him, after a particularly heated practice one day while I was taking care of the team, why he felt some of the players he had recruited were never going to make it in the NBA and why he wasn't afraid to let them know it.

Darryl put his catcher's mitt of a hand on my shoulder, looked me in the eyes, and said, "Man, it's not about the desire or even the skill of the player to make it to the NBA…it's a business and just like most businesses fail, the reality is, not everyone will make it no matter how hard they try or want it."

So if the athletes I was working with weren't shielded from failure and losing their identity, how could I be? I wished I had a coach telling me how it was so I could have been more prepared.

As fate would have it, prior to opening my first business, during a 16-month period, my life would change so drastically that there was nothing I could do but learn to cope and deal with stress, loss, and obstacles. My faith was tested and also deepened. Starting in the summer of 2002, I would end up getting divorced, moving from Pennsylvania to North Carolina, starting and then changing two different jobs, and then also losing my mother to lung cancer at the age of 56. I was lost, confused, challenged, and most of all scared. It felt like I was starting over again even though my life had only just begun.

It was ultimately during this time of self-discovery that I realized I had nothing to lose and everything to gain which gave me the courage to strike out on my own and open the business.

As I stood in the courtroom, my business closed and now facing personal bankruptcy, my mind raced. My emotions were somewhere between anger and too mentally and physically exhausted to care. The sleepless nights, the anguish of closing the doors on the thing I had spent almost every waking hour obsessing about over the last eight years, and the fact I had let down my wife and my boys, almost maniacally tortured me. Would our relationship be the same or would it change? Would they, my family, see me as a failure? With so many thoughts and no answers, I felt lost.

Yet the reality was, everything I had gone through already had set me up for dealing with tough times. I was now ready for dealing with the emotions, for dealing with the search to become better, for deepening my relationships with others. My experience would teach me what I wanted from my next business and how to be smarter the next time around.

I will often tell my running clients the story of Mary Decker Slaney and her quest for gold in the 1500m race in the 1984 Olympics. Arguably the greatest US female middle-distance runner ever, Decker Slaney was an odds-on favorite to win gold that Olympics, and yet an "accidental trip" by another opponent in the race caused her to fall and never finish. Even after her defeat caused by something out of her control, and despite injuries, surgeries, and obstacles, Decker Slaney was able to continue her career and move on. I felt the same way with the need to move on after my "fall," and I now teach my clients to do the same.

Ultimately, the decision to close the practice and file bankruptcy was multifactorial, most of it out of my control. Decisions had been made to expand the practice just prior to the worst recession in my lifetime, and taking on additional debt as the economy was about to contract was just poor timing. The business survived another four years, but closing it was the best decision under the circumstances.

I had taken a risk and learned very valuable life lessons because of it. In Rick Warren's book, *The Purpose Driven Life*, one of the lessons he provides is that your life message includes your life lessons. I learned many lessons from the whole experience.

I learned you don't need to be in the perfect financial position to be able to help others. I learned that failing does not mean you are a failure. I learned that I had a family which not only needed me but needed me to be at my best. And I learned that my clients needed me to be me. My overly optimistic self who could see the bright side of all situations including an injury or illness and could instill a sense of confidence that they too would get through the challenges they were facing.

As I look back at all I went through, I know the experience only made me a stronger and better businessman today. For me, it has never been about the money. Filing for bankruptcy is nothing to take lightly but is sometimes a necessary end to a business lifecycle. My family and I are doing great now, and I continue to practice physical therapy. I currently work with businesses and individuals to save money on health care related spending.

My real passion, however, is helping runners age 35-55 years old to run painlessly and be in their best health as they age. I'm big on education, so I use a podcast and a YouTube channel to educate runners on things they can do at home to relieve running related aches and pains. From my website, I provide virtual coaching for runners and have an online store for health and wellness related products.

In the end, I now realize it is possible to do good, despite not always doing well in life and in business and that, no matter what, my purpose of helping others is only strengthened because of my experiences and the lessons I learned.

TWEETABLE
You don't need to be in the perfect financial position to be able to help others.

Brian Boyle PT, DPT is a doctor of physical therapy, business owner, and coach. Dr. Brian is an expert working with WorkWell Prevention and Care to help large employers reduce injuries and save bottom line expenses on healthcare spending in the workplace. Dr. Brian also works with individuals through Company5k, a leading health and wellness company specializing in keeping runners and fitness enthusiasts over the age of 35 healthy and at their best. Dr. Brian can be reached by email at brian@company5k.com and found on Instagram @the_brian_boyle, on YouTube @MeshTongue, and on Anchor.fm, Run Painless.

CHAPTER 29
The Missed Kick

by Jason Ricks

I t is that moment you've dreamt about since you were a kid. There is under a minute left in the fourth quarter with a chance to kick a go-ahead field goal to seal the game against your hometown, the Texas Longhorns. 2007, Primetime, ABC. Packed Stadium. Left hash field goal under 40 yards. All eyes are on you.

The energy before a game-winning kick can be felt, and a frantic buzz reverberates throughout the stadium. A rare few people ultimately want my job during these moments. I thought I lived for these moments. It's said pressure does weird things to people. I can tell you it exposes you—any fear will be on full display and manifested. In these moments, you have to be present, relaxed, and confident. None of these exist without presence: living in the moment.

You think: *Routine, routine, routine. You've done this tens of thousands of times. Your leg is good, it's good. Trust it, you have one more in you. Make this f**king kick and beat the Longhorns! You got this!*

You take your steps, breathe, nod to your holder. There's the snap, hold, kick, all perfectly synchronized in under 1.35 seconds from snap to kick.

It's almost an out of body experience, and in a moment, it's gone. A routine kick is missed wide right. Life comes flooding back to you. You notice all of your senses at once but intensified. It's jarring. A high moment turns equally low in seconds. There's weight in that moment. Time is funny.

Failure comes washing over you as everyone in the stadium gasps. Disbelief and the ensuing shame for letting down your team settles in. The pain felt is unbearable. The gravity of the moment is so encompassing that others around you don't know how to act. Teammates, coaches, and media are at a loss for words, but their expressions speak volumes. Only a select few can actually muster the energy to make an attempt at condolence.

Instantly, I think about all the hard work, the countless hours training, rehabbing, and battling to get to this moment. How did I get to this place?

I was a nationally ranked kicker that started as a freshman, battled back from injury to recapture my starting possession, and was voted a captain. I was a Lou Groza watch list kicker heading into my junior year after kicking a game-winning field goal in the last seconds of the Independence Bowl against Alabama. An NFL prospect had been watching me kick in practice. My dreams had been manifesting in front of my eyes at 21 years old. What happened to me?

That was the last kick I ever attempted in a game, and it was my greatest teacher. It exposed me and was the moment I finally learned that my philosophy towards life up to this point had been flawed. Ironically, I knew before even playing the game that this would probably be my last. I reinjured my kicking leg and had a tear in my groin. Instead of removing myself from the game to prevent further damage, the coaching staff and I decided it would be best to take a pain killing injection shot to dull the pain. That decision was purely for my ego, which had fueled everything for me up to that point in my life.

I thought if I worked harder than anyone, physically training longer and more frequently, getting stronger, and doing it all by myself for myself, I would always succeed. I put more pressure on performance to mask my insecurities of fear. I didn't let anyone in to help deal with these issues, so they compounded in a negative way. This affected my mental-emotional state of being, which in turn wreaked havoc on my body and athletic career.

My friends and I discuss this approach as "redlining," as to say, going through life recklessly at 100 mph without the ability to see anything while leaving a mess behind you. Eventually, the engine has to breakdown and will need either a major repair or replacement. In my case, my body broke down through injury, and my fears consumed me. It was time for a change in philosophy, and simultaneously, the end of my athletic career.

You can't chase greatness, you can only focus on doing great work in the present moment. One of my favorite coaches used to say to me while I was going through the recruiting process, "Jason, don't worry. Keep doing great things and they (college programs) will find you." In other words, don't worry about things you can't control, and just keep doing what you are doing. The rest will take care of itself. He was right. Only through presence can you be "great." Fear of not being good enough, failing, and not achieving your dreams is living outside of the present moment. You decide if you're going to let fear of failure outweigh the joy and passion of the game. This is a conscious choice we get to pick every moment. Will you let the fear of a future moment or negative past event hold you back? Or, will your passion or that thing you love drive you? Which will win out is up to you. Ray Dalio's book *Principles* describes this choice well, "Imagine that in order to have a great life you have to cross a dangerous jungle. You can stay safe where you are and have an ordinary life, or you can risk crossing the jungle to have a terrific life. How would you approach that choice?"

If you're afraid of failure, you will never grow. And, if you think you won't fail, you've already lost. How can you reach your greatest heights without failure? You can't. So, you have to change your mindset around failure. Think about building a muscle. During training, you actually break down the muscle fibers, and if properly fed through sound nutrition, the body will repair these muscles to be stronger and bigger so the next time you lift you can lift a greater weight. You have to keep upping the weight to achieve your furthest potential. However, if you lift the same weight each workout, you'll never know that potential.

As a former track athlete, I love watching Usain Bolt and Michael Johnson. These guys smashed records and ran times that experts believed would never be obtained. Usain and Michael thought differently, and they not only changed the game but did it with joy and passion. Now that they have raised the bar, other athletes are running faster than ever. What happened? Are they taking steroids? Some new training? Nope, their minds have expanded, and they believe it can be done now. This is the power of the mind and belief.

Challenges and failure give us our depth, and they expand us if we provide the proper mindset. However, it's not easy to grow, and we like to feel comfortable. We don't want to lose what we have, so we rest on our laurels. Just keep embracing the discomfort as a sign you're challenging yourself in a healthy way. Be excited about the growth and don't let the fear of failure outweigh your excitement.

The feeling of my greatest failure I wouldn't wish on anyone. Massive failure or a significant life-changing event can shake the foundation of our belief system. In my case, my reality, ego, and value system came crashing down. This low point not only elicited the opportunity for a momentum shift, but also gave me the necessary room to reflect on my fears.

What I didn't realize is that everyone fails, and you may believe the pain you feel is unbearable, but you can make it through. Your success and growth depend on this. The pain took me years to recover from, and I disguised this discomfort in different unhealthy strategies that acted as a self-defense mechanism because it was the safe and comfortable thing to do. The only way to overcome this is to have the courage to go through it and address it. I was scared of letting down my team, being embarrassed, not being a part of the team, and not being good enough in life. What's behind all that fear?

The fear of not being loved by others. When I came to this realization, that hole inside me started to subside, and it left room around it. Interestingly, once you're on the other side, you may see things differently. Be open to new opportunities, and creativity may arise.

For me, I fell in love with real estate and investing out of nowhere. I couldn't stop absorbing information. It's like I had been starved and I had an all you can eat buffet in front of me. I was learning and putting myself out there again for the first time and making a ton of mistakes in the process. Learning, building, failing, and growing stronger, repeat! I went from one small deal to a one million dollar deal to +$10 million deals, one lease to 50 to +800 leases, a portfolio of three properties to running a portfolio in the hundreds of millions of dollars.

Ray Dalio in *Principles* says it best, "Life distributes tragedy indiscriminately, but only a few leverage the tragedy as a springboard for something far greater." I took everything I learned through my experiences and applied it to a far greater purpose. I realized that my passion can add great value to my partners, which will have a far greater impact on their lives than kicking a ball through the uprights. My value allows others to have space and time to spend as they please, which is far more important. Time is valuable, and it's the greatest resource we have. I've seen friends, family, and colleagues work incredibly hard in their job in order to make a living for themselves, but they give their soul for the safety of a paycheck.

I choose to work hard at my job but even harder on myself. Build equity, pay yourself first, and help others. Time and living a happy life are more important than money, but money helps to provide options: options to retire on your terms and time table and provide more financial security so you can spend more time with friends and family. I want my partners and I to live a life on our terms. Hopefully, this will allow them the space to find their passion to help others as well. That's my goal, and real estate (specifically, retail shopping centers) is just the vehicle to provide this.

So, my greatest teacher was my biggest failure. It exposed my flawed philosophy, and I lost interest in the nonmaterial ego-bound identity I created, which was nothing but a valueless mirage. I decided to live a life full of passion and address fears head-on in the moment, which I found leads to "success." What is success? It's having the desire, discipline, and determination to be the person you want to be and not have fears dictate your life. Don't give up and fail well.

TWEETABLE
You decide if you're going to let fear of failure outweigh the joy and passion of the game. This is a conscious choice we get to pick every moment.

Jason Ricks is a professional real estate investor, certified commercial investment member (CCIM), and syndicator with extensive experience in retail real estate. With his +10 years of experience in real estate, he oversees a portfolio in the hundreds of millions and acquires and enhances value-add retail properties across the country. His mission is to help others find financial freedom through retail investment. To connect with him by email or on LinkedIn.

Jason.ricks85@gmail.com
https://www.linkedin.com/in/ricksjason/

CHAPTER 30
Project Happiness

by Sarah Kim

I couldn't sleep. It was almost 3am, and I was staring at the ceiling fan as it cast darker shades of shadow on the walls of the room with a near-silent hum. That's when it hit me. My life was spinning out of control.

I surged out of bed perplexed and in tears. What am I doing with my life? What is my purpose for being here?

I searched for answers. I needed some clarity. I wanted someone or something to tell me what to do. I knew what I desired but was unsure how to get there.

Trying to be perfect and doing the right thing to please others is how I was raised. That mindset stuck with me for a long time and caused many emotional, mental, and even physical issues. I was never good enough. Feeling that way leaked into all areas of my life. I was always trying to be good enough. But for who?

I was born in Northern Virginia to South Korean immigrant parents. I lived a privileged life in a picturesque suburb with my little sister and brother. My father's business was booming, and my mother spent her days looking after us. My summers were filled with piano lessons, violin lessons, art class, book reports, and homework assignments my parents made-up. If you know anything about the Korean culture, you know how tough it can be. For business reasons, we moved to Charlotte, NC where there was very little diversity at the time. I grew up feeling isolated because I looked different from the other girls. I didn't speak English until the age of seven. When I started school in the first grade, I couldn't relate to any of my classmates. I was immersed in American culture. I quickly started to rebel against my parents. I remember once telling my father in anger, "If you want me to simply be subservient, you should have raised me in South Korea."

For reasons never fully explained, my parents divorced. That is when things dramatically changed for me. For most of my childhood, I had attended a private Christian school with my siblings. Then, seemingly overnight, I was enrolled in a public school. Alone. Without my siblings.

We went from the rich Asian family to a broke, broken family. There was no explanation. Only shame. In that moment, my certainty of safety had been shaken. I was no longer confident in my place in this world, and worse, who I was.

In the middle of high school, I moved from North Carolina to Virginia where my father lived. As I got older, my parents always compared me to their friends' children and lamented how so and so's child went to this university and why I couldn't do what they were doing. They believed the key to happiness was to go to school, get a good job, and marry a good husband. They weren't grooming me to have a good life. They were grooming me to be a good wife. But what they wanted for me wasn't what I wanted for myself.

A friend of mine was doing very well selling new home construction while I was entering college, and that is when I made a decision to get my license to sell. My father did not want me to get into that field. He would say anyone could be a "realtor," and that I was better than that since he wanted me to finish school to get my bachelor's. He was not thrilled when I decided to sell real estate after college.

Later, as an adult, I would still not be good enough for my parents as a top-producing real estate agent who was debt free. I had paid off all my student loans, purchased my first BMW, and moved out of the house. After graduation, I was determined to live a fulfilling and purposeful life. I just didn't know what that would look like. Years before, my father had made a choice to improve our family. Now, he was beyond frustrated that I was trying to improve myself with the career path I had chosen.

I took what they said with a grain of salt and followed what my heart was telling me to do. Turns out, real estate was my passion. I enjoyed helping and educating others through real estate. I was a top producer with Keller Williams my first year, making six figures, and my income has only grown since then.

Even though things seemed great, I did not feel successful. I was not able to celebrate my victories and pushed forward to do more and be more. I measured my success by how much money I made, what I drove, where I lived, and what I had. I was left empty year after year. But there is a difference between being successful and having a sense of achievement. For a long time I walked this life simply existing and trying to avoid any pain. I was miserable. I knew I had to change something and do something different. All I knew was that I did not want to continue this feeling of emptiness.

I had to quit believing the lies I told myself about who I was and quit living the shallow image of what others painted me to be. I questioned myself constantly and sought validation from others. I wanted to know that I was good enough.

It was time for a mental shift that had been years in development. I have been searching for my life's purpose from such a young age and have made significant discoveries about myself in my journey. The year I was in college and living with my best friend, around my 21st birthday, I quit drinking alcohol and started focusing on mindfulness to get to know myself. It has been an amazing journey getting to know who I am and who I want to become. I have strived to be the best version of myself daily. You could say that I found God that year.

Once I decided to stop living in my own inner melodrama and started surrounding myself with situations which stimulated growth, my life was completely transformed. I became obsessed with mindfulness, learning how to meditate and attracting positive energy everywhere I went. I had to unlearn all the self-doubt and re-train my subconscious mind. We all have some sort of trauma in our lives. We can only control how we choose to move forward from it. I had to kick out my inner roommate who kept telling me that I was not good enough. Once I did that, my life changed.

I heard once that the prerequisite to true freedom is to decide that you do not want to suffer anymore. I had decided that I did not want to suffer anymore, but I got stuck. My life was unchanging for quite some time. I grew frustrated. I slipped back into what I thought my life path was supposed to look like. Perhaps getting married and having a child would make me happy.

Even though my brief marriage didn't work out, my son is a blessing and in a way so was my marriage. I learned a lot about myself that I wouldn't have if I never married. I eventually realized that I was only treating my symptoms by covering them up and not actually getting to the root of them. I was always stressed because I had given my mind an impossible task: to protect me from all sadness, anger, fear, and heartbreaks. My mind was too active and overloaded trying to protect myself. I had to learn how to deal with my C-PTSD (complex trauma disorder). I had to learn to release all my insecurities and fears. I had to learn to relax.

Life is a roller coaster, and I had to figure out how to respond and not react. I had to know who I truly was and how I wanted to be remembered once I left this earth. I constantly questioned myself: *Who am I?* Once I figured out who I was, I was able to bulletproof myself from the outside world. I made a conscious decision that I would be happy no matter what life threw at me. I asked myself: *What are my values? What do I offer? What is my vision? How do I want to live my life? What does my heart desire the most? What type of people do I want to attract?* I no longer lived my life in fear of failure. I was no longer trying to constantly protect myself from feeling pain by controlling my environment to avoid any suffering.

I no longer tie my success to material goods or hide behind other people. I no longer compare myself to others. I learned that you first have to accept people for who they are. You don't have to like them or spend time with them. People don't know what they don't know. I had to accept my parents for who they are and love them wholeheartedly just as they are. I could no longer visit the past of endless spankings and book reports my parents made me do. They did the best they could and raised us the only way they knew how. My parents lived in a different era. I learned to respect them and accept them as they are.

I learned you don't have to be liked by everyone. I have to continuously work on myself and invest the most in myself because we cannot help others until we are fully capable of being the best we can be as a person. As the great motivational speaker Jim Rohn said, "The greatest gift you can give someone else is your own personal development."

Growing up, I cared what other people thought of me. Appearances were everything. I wanted to be liked. I was easily influenced and did not know how to make good decisions as a young adult. Even today, choosing what makes me happy and what I think is best for my son and me is not always easy. I have to consciously block out when others tell me what is right for me and my life. People will judge you for your decisions, but I quickly learned that it doesn't matter. I know what's right for us. I only take advice from my inner circle who are where I'd like to be.

The real me came out when it was hiding in the deep for so long, waiting to be re-discovered. I'm no longer just skimming the surface, I'm breaking through to success.

TWEETABLE
It is in those moments that feel like death that our truest potential is born. Listen to what makes your heart happy and use that as your compass. In our pain we find our greatest power!

Sarah Kim is a business and marketing strategist with a passion for helping others find financial freedom through real estate investing. Sarah is currently building an online coaching course to help others dream, believe, and achieve their full potential.

Sarah is most excited about building a family legacy.

Contact: 571-310-5353 | realtorsarahkim@gmail.com

CHAPTER 31

The Happiest Man in Texas

by Victor Awtry

To you baby boomers out there who wake up like I do with a new ache or pain everyday...here are a few words of affirmation and consolation. **You are never too old to be happy, and you should never give up on love.**

I am truly blessed and so thankful to have become the one and only happiest man in Texas. However, I do realize I cannot take the credit for this milestone alone. I know in my heart this has only happened to me because of my amazing wife Debby, my truly splendid five daughters, everyone's friend—Ms. Ann, and last and least my digital "mistress."

All of these incredible ladies have changed my life for the better. My daughters, now all married, shelter their families with high moral values of honesty, compassion, empathy, and kindness. It truly humbles me to observe the energy and intensity with which they care for themselves, their families, and their communities. I have tried in my own fumbling way to show my ladies the awe and pride I feel observing their steadfast resolve to nurture the life around them. Their energy for doing the right thing for everyone compels me to want to be that better man, that better father and better grandfather that I should be.

Sadly, I was not intelligent enough to provide the smoothest glide path for my daughters to grow up on. You see, apparently their father has a tendency to marry to the tune of that Coldplay song that goes "I will fix you." As we say in Texas, that dog won't hunt and never has. So, without a reliable female role model in our Southlake home, my mother Marie selflessly stepped up to make certain our girls grew up well. My daughters are, of course, all different and like every human have their own personal challenges, but I can only feel the deepest satisfaction for the honor of being their dad.

My girls are smart, savvy, and successful at whatever they want to do. Their strength of character and the energetic intensity with which they seek fairness and empathy for others warms my heart that I must have done something right. I was a single dad for many years, so it would be remiss and wrongheaded not to acknowledge that many other kind women stepped up to take my girls shopping, be a friend, and hear them in ways a dad cannot or should not. While I have tried to thank all these ladies over the years, and I pray they know who they are, one special lady named Ann (married to a high school buddy of mine) deserves special appreciation from the Awtry's for her compassion, empathy, and wisdom.

A dear priest friend of mine once told me "Don't give up on love." I thought *Yeah...right.*

So, while my beautiful daughters have elevated me from being **happy** to being **happier**, I know they too are astonished and delighted to see my new incredible wife Ms. Debby propel my leap into being the **happiest** man in Texas.

My Debby is truly the perfect woman for me. From our first "interview" date courtesy of Match.com, I knew she was different. I will admit that when she told me she had seven grown children, I did unconsciously take three mental steps back and put my hands in my pockets to find my car keys. She saw this, yet sweetly and gently pointed out to me that while she had seven children all grown, mature, and independent, she only had three daughters to my five!

The more we talked, I learned Debby had lived and worked on a Chicago area farm for years, and that she had homeschooled her wonderful children with one being accepted to the Air Force Academy. She cooked organically, cleaned meticulously, and ground her own wheat to cook homemade bread. She had loved her life as a mother and a teacher. Ms. Debby, my wife who is to me holy and full of grace, is also incredibly creative and teaches quilting and knitting at her Mountain Laurel Retreat for women in New Braunfels. I am humbled with the realization that after being single for 13 years, I was blessed to find the most caring, thoughtful person I have ever met in my life. I often wonder how such a wonderfully earthy, talented woman could choose a man like me. Most of my day is in front of a computer trying to help baby boomers and millennials achieve their dream of having their own Shopify store. My daily prayer is that my Debby's simple and pure life will compliment my often online virtual one. I hope to make it into heaven on her coattails.

My sweetie is not only a friend to me, she also inspires me with her compassion, kindness, and gentleness to do what I always thought a husband would be obligated to do for his wife and mother in their latter years—put that good wife up on a pedestal of respect for the years of work mothers and all great ladies do. While I was not the father of her seven children, I know it is right and just for me to place my Debby on that pedestal she so deserves.

It has been wonderful for me, at the age of 68, to find myself enjoying a level of happiness and acceptance that seemed to be just out of my reach in my younger years. Like most of us, I guess I had always accepted the fact that aging would take me down a fairly predictable path of a slow mental decline. And, of course, aging would be coupled with a depressing inability to recall names and faces, or to get excited about new opportunities and new technologies which I love to fancy, or to realize a degree of wisdom about life.

I remember distinctly that January day in my mid 50s, looking in the mirror and thinking surely I was doomed to become that grouchy old granddaddy that at best my daughters and grandchildren might tolerate. I wanted not to be a source of ridicule but rather to be a blessing, maybe even a respected source of wisdom to them as C.S. Lewis so beautifully described it with the word "lovingkindness." Most of all, I wanted to be certain my daughters and grandchildren (still one or two more possible!) knew all the love I felt for them.

While I had done well enough in business, I am certainly not rich financially, but I always knew I would be fine having "enough." Early on, I understood that money does not make anyone happy and that all it can really do is make you comfortable.

Despite all the blessings, I found myself going into my 60s with the nagging unfulfilled desire to build a software company that was really out there on the cutting edge of technology. I knew having the kind of company I wanted would take long hours, hard work, and that I would have to risk it all. I knew I had to take the risk soon or I would go to my grave thinking I simply had not had enough faith in myself and my God, who I knew loved me. I felt myself in danger of not accomplishing what the good Lord sent me here to do. I was running out of runway.

Instead, to my delight, I discovered new skills and a new confidence. Once I made that first fateful leap, I was able to appreciate that the application of the good old American values of hard work and persistence still pays off.

Now, after years of investment and hard work, I have been blessed to watch my company iPersonalyze grow and become profitable, not only for me but also for my business partners and clients. The learning process I went through and all the holes I stepped in made it possible for me to give back to other entrepreneurs. I saw that during my journey I had learned some valuable insights I could teach and share. The technology business I unwisely had put on hold for so many years lives!

I have also learned why I think any baby boomer should take the leap and accept the risk to fulfill their own dream, their own passion they have been ignoring like I did. I believe our brains are wired to help us baby boomers!

With a little research, I have learned that neurologists now believe our brains, instead of starting down a path of slow decline after middle age and fogging up little by little until our 70s or 80s, can mature. And with some focused personal effort, new learning will inevitably bring new cognitive skills online. These new skills, enabled by neurons hooking up with new, significant others, cross-index with each other as we age. The pleasing result is that our existing experiences and knowledge combine in exciting new ways.

This makes sense to me. I am certainly not a neurologist, but I can logically relate a brain to a computer. I recognize that my short-term memory, like a computer's RAM, is unable to pack huge new gigabytes of raw data into it. Even so, its years of accumulated mental bits and bytes of experience and knowledge are somehow more accessible than ever before!

Neurologists also tell us that we acquire better reasoning skills in middle age as fresh layers of myelin sheath are laid down in our brain. Essentially, it appears that well before we really get into our 60s, our brains have spent decades upgrading themselves from a simple dial up connection to a high speed fiber optic version.

So, while short-term memory and retention decline because our short-term RAM store is full, our ability to access and recompile what we already know grows if you challenge yourself by going out and taking risks.

So, the launching of my digital love, my "mistress," iPersonalyze in my 60s, has helped me encourage those old neurons floating around in my hard drive to locate new, significant neurons to give me new insights. I believe this process is not only mentally healthy for us as we enter our later years, but it is also a golden opportunity to experience the satisfaction of seeing latent creative skills emerge. And better yet, with these new skills and connections kicking in, we get wiser with improved ability to parse meanings and manage information.

I believe any mental leaps one can take are leaps of growth and blessing that are built into our brain chemistry by our Creator, who is "lovingkindness" itself.

The even better news for us baby boomers is that I am pretty sure that becoming **happy**, **happier**, and the **happiest** is not even the best end we can achieve. For I have noticed that on those rare occasions when I am honestly humble and truly forgiving with a thankful heart, I can catch a glimpse of the next mental leap coming online soon—**peace and joy**.

Certainly it is a bit bodacious, even when writing in Texan, for any man to categorically state that he is *THE* happiest man anywhere. However, it seems logical that someone in Texas must be the happiest, and since now I have all this newfound confidence via my improved neurons, I see no reason why I should not stake my claim to being the happiest. Truthfully, with all the love that surrounds me I cannot fathom how any Texan could be happier. Actually, I hope many more claim to be...and at the same time recognize their own thankfulness.

So, boomers out there, please take heart. Launch that business, search for new ideas, and share your own new wisdom as you cross the finish line of this good race. Yes, your bodies are starting to suck it up. It happens. But, the fantastically great news is that your Creator still loves you and from time eternal engineered your brain to help you become the best you could ever be and the happiest you have ever been in your life.

TWEETABLE

It is a bit bodacious for any man to state that he is *THE* happiest man anywhere. But, I see no reason why I should not stake my claim. With all the love that surrounds me, I cannot fathom how any Texan could be happier.

Victor Awtry is a visionary entrepreneur and founder and CEO of iPersonalyze. As innovative and creative software developer, Victor seeks to bring the latest cutting edge personalization technologies, typically available to only larger companies, down to smaller companies and startups in the graphics, printing, and communication industries. Victor is regarded by his peers as a thought leader in the emerging Fourth Wave of Mass Customization, which Victor renames Mass Personalization since customization is about products and personalization is about people.

1308 East Common Street, New Braunfels, TX 78130

817.329.6621, 817.938.3305 cell

CHAPTER 32

Financial Success to Financial Freedom

Finding Your Why

by Derek Baker

"You're raising a comedian" is what my parents were told at parent teacher conferences by my middle school science teacher. Needless to say, school did not captivate my attention. On most days you could find me goofing off during class. I liked having fun, making people laugh, and being the life of the party. I was raised by two loving parents that taught my brother and I to be honest, hardworking men. They taught us the definition of success was going to school in which I learned to apply myself to get good grades in order to get into a good college which would allow us to get a good job and a comfortable life.

Since the fifth grade I wanted to become a mechanical engineer and design cars for the automotive industry. I was born in Flint, Michigan, and to say the automotive industry was in my blood would be an understatement. My grandfather, father, brother, plus numerous aunts, uncles, and cousins all work or have retired from the auto industry. Many years later when I did become the mechanical engineer designing cars that I had always dreamed of, I quickly discovered it wasn't everything I had imagined it to be. I wasn't designing the entire car, I was actually designing a small piece of the car people would never actually see. Since I was an employee, I was also being told what to do. I worked for "the man" (or woman) and never really enjoyed that. It strips a person's mind of creativity when you are told what to do, when you are given boundaries.

My high school sweetheart, Amy, and I got married, bought a house, and were living the life of dual income with no kids. We were comfortable and started on a financial glide path that would provide us an upper middle-class life.

Some years passed before Amy and I decided it was time to start the next chapter in our lives and grow our family. May 1, 2015 was the day my life changed forever, and my mindset began to shift. As I looked at this little 7lb 11oz girl named Molly, I stopped thinking of myself and started to think about how I was going to provide the world to this new baby. Becoming a parent for the first time can have an incredible impact on your life. We started looking at the future. *How can we make it so Amy can be a full-time mom? How are we going to pay for Molly's college? How can we show our children the world and what is really important in life? And what about that dream house we have always talked about?* Our once financially successful careers didn't feel so cushy anymore. There had to be something that we were not considering, so we began reaching out to our peers. How were they dealing with these similar struggles? We learned that they were dealing by making sacrifices and that we would need to prioritize what was important because the path we were on did not fulfill our ultimate desires. Amy and I just could not shake this feeling that there had to be more. There had to be a way to allow for Amy to stay at home and still have the luxuries that we have grown to know while saving for our future. But how? Everyone in our network was playing it safe and this is what we were raised to do. This was all we had known.

In the meantime, Amy began working part-time. Since she is an engineer too, it was extremely difficult to justify her quitting altogether because family had volunteered to watch Molly on her work days. Amy and I are so very blessed to have such amazing parents and siblings who have helped develop a strong network and foundation for our children. We began listening to audiobooks to and from work instead of just filling our two-hour commute with music or talk radio. During this time, we discovered several helpful resources and people who were doing what we thought was the impossible.

A 207-page book would change our whole frame of mind: *Rich Dad, Poor Dad* by Robert Kiyosaki. This book transformed our entire perspective and outlook on life. We learned that what we needed more than financial success was financial freedom. When this day comes, I will no longer be working for money, money will be working for me. That morning, as we lined up to swipe our badges into the building and walk through the revolving doors for work, we found how true Robert Kiyosaki's words resonated with us, and our need for financial freedom became stronger than ever. We immediately realized how our education had taught us to be great employees and climb the corporate ladder, sacrificing our precious time with our kids for money. As Tony Gaskins said, "If you don't build your dream, someone will hire you to help build theirs." I find great motivation in this quote and use it to fuel my commitment to my goals and my family.

Now that we had found what we were looking for, it was time to take action. With no real estate background or education, I started listening to books, watching videos, and listening to podcasts. I was hell-bent on learning the world of real estate, and it consumed all of my free time. We looked at single-family rental houses to purchase and rent. We looked at buying underperforming mortgage notes. We even looked at renting houses and turning them into Airbnbs. We had a burning desire to do something but realized each of these options required an extended period of time and scalability in order to see a benefit. We discovered Grant Cardone and Michael Blank through YouTube, and they both were teaching multifamily apartment investing. I was hooked. It really made the most sense, and historically it outperforms the stock market with less volatility. In April of 2016, we founded Jamtine Investments where we focus on apartment (multifamily) real estate investing to reach our financial freedom goals.

Multifamily is not a sector of real estate that a person can jump right into. To be good, it requires a large amount of training and experience plus obtaining a strong network. While I focused on educating myself by studying the market, underwriting deals, and attending conferences and meetups, Amy and I worked to build our savings. This period of time taught me patience. I was anxious to jump right into a deal but knew from other's experiences it was critical to have the proper execution take place because if anything were to be overlooked it could become a costly mistake.

We had two criteria for our first deal. It had to be close to home so we could gain first-hand experience and big enough to have a property management company oversee the day to day activities. Once I had become very proficient at underwriting deals, I began to feel stagnant and discouraged. I was not the first call on brokers lists, and websites such as LoopNet generally didn't provide deals where the numbers made sense. Amy and I have always had faith that God has a plan for us and that it is all in His timing, not ours. This period became a true testament to that belief. However, God does open doors when you place your faith in Him. We found a C-class, 23-unit apartment complex that was 1.5 hours away on Craigslist of all places! The feeling of excitement I had when I signed on the 23-unit apartment complex gave me an even stronger desire to take control over my future and the feeling that anything is possible.

I was very excited to share this new adventure with our support system, our family and friends. We received a lot of mixed emotions. This was something new, something crazy. My whole life I was taught do not fail, play it safe, and don't get hurt. For the first time in my life, I was going against the grain and the opinions of the role models in my life. I am a numbers guy and knew what I had done made sense. God again provided me with the strength and support when I needed it and has given me a new mentor for this area in my life.

I am learning that without big risks comes little reward. Stepping outside of your comfort zone is where life really begins. With two daughters and a son on the way, my WHY is stronger than ever, and I am determined to reach the goals I have set for our family and to leave a legacy to our children. I recently heard in an interview that billionaire entrepreneur Sara Blakely was asked by her father at dinner each week, "What have you failed at this week?" How great is that? That is far from how most parents would start a dinner conversation. This is something I will instill in my children. I will encourage them to think outside of the box, push themselves out of their comfort zone, and not be afraid to try new things and take risks.

After acquiring the 23-unit apartment building and developing the first-hand experience of multifamily apartment ownership, Amy and I decided we were ready to expand our minds and think bigger through multifamily syndication. I joined Mark and Tamiel Kenney's Think Multifamily team because of the values they live and do business by. They attract a special group of people that we call Family Syndication. Being surrounded by like-minded people that understand and support your dream gives you power to succeed. My fire inside has been ignited, and I found a desire, a calling in life that is stronger than ever before. Being driven by a force greater than yourself is a powerful source of energy that no one can stop, no one can slow down. So, find your WHY, stay focused on your dreams, and believe in yourself. Your life is your story, so you write it.

TWEETABLE

Motivation drives desire. Find out what motivates you, hold on to it, nurture it. Wake up each day with a purpose to become a better you. Stay determined to succeed and follow your heart.

Derek Baker is a real estate investor, entrepreneur, and principal and founder of Jamtine Investments who owns and manages a rental portfolio of 23 multifamily units. His mission is to provide an opportunity for people to achieve their path to financial freedom through passive real estate investments. Derek enjoys spending time with his family, fly fishing, golf, and his alma mater, Michigan State University. Derek is the husband to his wife Amy of seven years and father to three amazing children Molly, Emma, and Brayden.

Connect directly with Derek and learn more about multifamily investing and his team.

Email: Derek@Jamtineinvestments.com

www.jamtineinvestments.com

CHAPTER 33

Ikigai

A Reason for Being

by Brian & Tracey Akamine

kigai is a Japanese concept meaning a reason for being.

It occurs with the converging of four factors:

1. Your passion or what you love to do
2. Your skill sets and what you're good at
3. Your mission and what the world needs, and
4. Your vocation for which you can be paid by doing it.

When one or more of these factors is missing, however, the results are either:

1. Delight and fullness, but no wealth
2. Excitement and complacency, but a sense of uncertainty
3. Satisfaction, but feelings of uselessness, or
4. Comfortable, but feelings of emptiness.

However, when these four factors converge, that's where Ikigai "our reason for being" begins.

Isn't that what we all desire? A reason for being?

Over a span of two decades, we discovered our Ikigai.

After praying *Let our heart be broken by the things that break the heart of God*, a radical shift in our mindset occurred. But it was a process. Painful, but worth it. It required an unrelenting desire, determination, and discipline to find that converging center.

There is power in this understanding of mindset. We become co-creators. We have discovered what John Maxwell describes as having a *"purpose with a divine touch."*

Our life together as transformational leaders has been a journey of discovering our Ikigai. Imagine two individuals striving and thriving to become the best version of ourselves individually and together.

Since that prayer, we've experienced and witnessed incredible impacts made in the lives of hundreds if not thousands of people resulting from a bold risk-taking choice to take action.

We left a very comfortable Southern California lifestyle, great weather, beautiful beaches, great friends, quality of life, nice cars, a house, flourishing careers, etc., to respond to a calling to move to the East coast to plant churches and minister among the least, the lost, and lonely near the cities of New York and Philadelphia.

We started a new church, served in both small and large church staffs, led and strengthened organizational capacity for several non-profit organizations, organized and mobilized thousands of volunteers providing food, clothing, furniture, and shelter for the displaced and homeless. We modeled healthy family systems, provided a parenting program for at-risk families and those released from prisons, organized community leaders to create social change, advocated for the disenfranchised, and became a catalyst connecting resources between the haves and the have-nots. All these experiences were a result of an answered prayer and burning desire to see God transform people's lives.

It took determination and grit to persevere through many obstacles, disappointments, heartaches, politics, and setbacks along the way. It required discipline in our lifestyle and standard of living while encouraging one another to persevere to fuel our reason for being, the calling to minister to the underserved and marginalized. Who would have known that eventually our determination to serve others would one day be commended by a Pennsylvania state senator as a shining example of community spirit? We were told our many contributions were worthy of deep gratitude and respect because of our dedication and excellence contributing to the well-being of our community.

What might appear to be a positive outcome from our desire to serve others did not come without a price. Literally. Financially speaking, we always found ourselves struggling to sustain ourselves. Expenses exceeded inconsistent sources of income. We soon discovered that depending on tithes, offerings, grants, and donations was always volatile for us, subject to and dependent upon terms and conditions, or the politics of distributed funding. This dependency left us in debt and stressed mentally, physically, and financially. There is a common saying in ministry: find the need and fill it. This notion is also dependent upon finding those who will fund it. This is where every social entrepreneur discovers what either makes or breaks you. Funding in the non-profit sector is often cyclical and volatile.

We repeatedly experienced financial impasses. Remember the four circles of Ikigai? We were excelling at three of four circles. We knew we had the passion, skillset, and social capacity. We knew what the needs were, and we were quite effectively meeting them, but the missing variable was the fourth circle, getting paid or funded to sustain us to do the other three areas well. It was like a four-legged table missing the fourth leg. Our lifestyle was unsustainable even though our core value was *live simple, so others may simply live.* Something had to give. Something was seriously wrong. It didn't make sense.

How was it that I could be so committed to a cause that was morally just—to advocate for the marginalized, to facilitate stakeholders to cooperate for the common good, to disrupt self-serving institutionalized systems that perpetuate and service poverty, crime, and drug-abuse and capitalize on the social ills of society—while I was having to work four to five part-time jobs to make ends meet for my family? The side jobs were pulling me away from my purpose, but I couldn't imagine myself working a full-time job and doing the ministry on the side. We didn't leave California to work a full-time job completely unrelated to why we left. We would have stayed in California to do that.

I felt defeated. There I was, one of influence, trusted among every level in the community, yet struggling financially. I was often called upon to be the go-to person to provide strategic community leadership among key stakeholders, who by the way, were employed full-time as service providers like those whom they represented.

At the end of the day, they could go home to their families and show up again in the morning. I on the other hand had to work multiple jobs and do the things I was doing "voluntary" or with minimal financial support for my time vested. It was not working for us. I would often pray, *Lord, my heart is broken for the things that matter to you, but we're drowning. Help us!* I then realized something. In our earnest desire, determination, and discipline to do what we were committed to, we painfully discovered that we were misguided in our thinking when it came to supporting the ministry. I have heard it said, the best way to help the poor is not to become one of them. At the core of our situation, we realized that it was a stewardship issue.

Remember what they say before take-off in an airplane: In case of emergency, for your safety and the safety of others, first, put on your oxygen mask before assisting others. Well, we realized that it was time to put on our oxygen mask.

Call it an answer to prayer or coming to our senses. How did we do it? An awakening occurred. A mindset-shift happened. Our context expanded.

I came across the book *Rich Dad, Poor Dad* by Robert Kiyosaki and had a profound awakening. Lesson number one: the rich don't work for money, money works for them. That simple principle changed my whole view of thinking and more. I had to deal with my distorted view of the word "rich." I equated it with the outcome of my father, an entrepreneur, who abandoned us in pursuit of greed and being rich. I had a distorted view because of the outcome he demonstrated in its pursuit. In actuality, being rich is a measure of time. Because money is time. People with lots of money have lots of time because they don't have to spend their life trading their time for money. Instead, they can trade their money for time.

We were trading our time for money. Our income was not keeping up with increasing expenses. Especially with aging parents, growing teenagers, my wife's health challenges, and my own well-being declining, we were tired of feeling tired. With a mindset of trading time for money and dependent on others for support to fund the ministry, we were both feeling stressed trying to manage a cleaning business, part-time jobs, and both of us serving in our passion for ministry.

The rich don't work for money because they invest in assets like real estate, commodities, or paper assets that produce passive income, or cash flow, which when leveraged correctly can produce infinite returns.

Kiyosaki's explanation of the Cashflow Quadrant unlocked our understanding of how taxes are your largest single expense. Tom Wheelwright's book *Tax-Free Wealth* starts with, "Taxes are stealing your money, your time, and your future. However, if you change your facts, you change your tax, and becoming an investor or business owner in real estate is the single most tax-saving strategy to build massive wealth by permanently lowering your taxes. The first thing you need to do is to increase your financial intelligence by investing in financial education."

I realized I had been sitting on some investment real estate for 30 years, and it was time to leverage an existing asset. I took immediate action to change my facts. I invested in my financial education through, Rich Dad coaching, ProVision Tax & Wealth Strategy, The Real Estate Guys Syndication Mentoring Club, and Brad Sumrok's Apartment Investors Mastery Foundations Program.

As our financial IQ increased, we knew our success would require a decision. It would require us to change our mindset and leverage what we already had in our possession. Zig Ziglar once said, "When obstacles arise, you change your direction to reach your goal. You do not change your decision to get there." We desired to change our direction but not our decision to our mission. As Tony Robbins said, "Stay committed to your decision, but stay flexible in your approach."

It was time to be flexible and refocus the core of our issue: our mindset. To recognize the tools and resources we had all along. We simply didn't see it.

I had to step back and recognize that it was not for us to spiritualize personal management issues and not for us to manage the spiritual realm as it relates to the supernatural. Discerning between the two was our journey.

We now recognized that we had a choice. If nothing changed, nothing would change. The moment we made a choice to change, supernatural intervention ushered in.

God would show us through personal transformation our reason for being. The key to the fourth missing leg of Ikigai is the "oxygen mask."

Our oxygen mask started through my wife's health journey.

The summer of 2012, when Tracey was just about to turn 50, life took us on an unexpected detour. Tracey had been doing her regular regimen of healthy eating and daily exercise. She was diagnosed with hypothyroidism.

Being a mom of two young girls, a business owner, and involved in her church community and children's school, she continued on her daily regimen, putting her health and pain on the back burner. Her symptoms multiplied. Her fatigue became unbearable, she had gained over 40 lbs., and the nagging back pain had driven her to various doctors for a medical diagnosis, all to no avail. After a battery of tests, exams, doctors, and specialists, no one could tell her what the source of her weight gain and discomfort were. Her endocrinologist also told her that her thyroid levels were in a good range and to continue the prescribed medication. By that following fall, after a stressful move and beginning a random hypothyroidism regimen found on the internet, Tracey was left in despair.

It was then that I looked at my once vibrant, healthy, and motivated wife and saw a shell of what she had been. I remember her saying that she felt as though she was dying. This was the intersection point of faith, desire, determination, and discipline.

Although Tracey had actually prayed for God to take her home if this was all there was for her, she also knew that God had planted good seed and great dreams in her heart to accomplish. She began visiting a holistic wellness clinic. Through whole food supplements and a whole food regime, she fully regained her vitality. Her clinician told her that she would lose the weight once her body was healed.

After two years of a strict regimen, although she felt much better, she could not shed even a pound. She saw her friend Janet on the internet talking about an optimal health program and the Habits of Health system designed by Dr. Wayne Anderson. After talking with her, she didn't want to commit to another plan and fail, so she fasted and prayed for 40 days. During that time, she gained four more pounds. With that, she called Janet and said, "I'll start your program." Her transformation was so amazing that people started to notice and ask how they could get the same results.

Because of her experience and results, she knew she couldn't keep this a secret, so she decided to pay it forward and become an OPTAVIA certified health coach. This is where the awakening happened. Her desire to regain her life, her determination to get healthy, and her discipline to make these lifestyle changes caused both she and I to gain so much more. She inspired me. When I went on the program, I lost 30 lbs. and regained my vitality to the extent of completing my third Ironman Triathlon after a 28-year hiatus of sedentary living. Together, our oxygen masks were back on.

We were finally dead set in the center of our Ikigai: a healthy mind, body, and now finally finances!

Our goal is to sit on the other side of the table to coach and empower future social entrepreneurs to find the need, fill it, and fund it. We believe we were awakened to the opportunity to live our best life, and more importantly, to share what we have learned with others.

Through our experiences in urban ministry, real estate investing, and health coaching, we now see through the lens of assisting others to live a transformed life with healthy mind, healthy body, healthy soul, and healthy finances.

> *"You can get everything you want in life, if you just help enough other people get what they want."*
>
> **– Zig Ziglar**

We would love for you to live an optimal life. After all, you only get one life, and we would love to partner with you to assist you in creating your best life ever with a missional purpose.

We want you to know, if we can do it you can do it too. We are ordinary people with an extraordinary mission. When you have a clear sense of calling, a desire and determination to do whatever it takes to sharpen your skills, the discipline to stay in the game, and a single focus on your course of action, the rest falls into place.

> *"If you work on your goals, your goals will go to work on you. If you go to work on your plan, your plan will go to work on you. Whatever good things we build end up building us."*
> **– Jim Rohn**

Our journey continues to take us through this convergence of discovering our Ikigai.

Fuel your desire, stay determined, lead from structure not emotion, and stay disciplined.

We challenge you to seek your Ikigai!

TWEETABLE
It was time to be flexible and refocus the core of our issue: our mindset. To recognize the tools and resources we had all along. We simply didn't see it.

Brian Akamine is an ordained minister, multifamily investor and syndicator, health coach, and three-time Ironman triathlete. Tracey Akamine is a health coach, speaker, entrepreneur, and published author. With 30 years real estate experience, they invest with ministry-minded individuals to reposition underperforming assets and revitalize B and C-class multifamily communities. As OPTAVIA certified health coaches, Tracey and Brian have transformed over 600 lives by supporting individuals to achieve their health goals. They love to inspire through speaking and one-on-one coaching. To contact, www.redpeakpartners.com. Email brian.akamine@redpeakpartners.com or tracey.akamine@redpeakpartners.com.

Facebook: https://www.facebook.com/brian.akamine.7 https://www.facebook.com/tracey.daleakamine

LinkedIn: https://www.linkedin.com/in/brian-akamine-b71a66170/

Zoom Room: https://zoom.us/j/6103081309

CHAPTER 34

Coach K. Was No Overnight Success

by Newy Scruggs

In the Kyle Wilson Inner Circle, we often talk about how things take time. Success is just not microwaved. Even so, today more so than ever, people want instant success. Like my seven-year-old, if we try something and we're not good at it right away, we think *I'm not good, I'm not good, I can't do it*. No, the truth is we have to work at it.

I grew up in North Carolina, and when you live in North Carolina, people ask you, who's your team? When I was younger, there were no pro teams like there are now, so when they asked who's your team, they meant college basketball. My team was North Carolina. Michael Jordan was playing there (before he was Michael Jordan). The second team that was really big in the state was the NC State Wolfpack. And then, it was Duke coached by Mike Krzyzewski.

Carolina fans hate Duke, but, as said in *The Art of War*, know your enemy. Mike was a great general. What he's done in his sport we won't see again. You won't see anyone last that long or be given the time needed to achieve what he achieved.

When Krzyzewski started coaching, Duke's team wasn't who they are today. Now they're a known brand, but back then it wasn't like that. They struggled, and at the time, Krzyzewski was coaching against Dean Smith, a legend at North Carolina, and Jim Valvano, a very colorful, electric personality, a guy that people just loved. Compared, Mike was the Polish guy who's name nobody could pronounce or spell. Dean Smith at North Carolina had won the national championship for Carolina in '81, and the next year Jim Valvano won it for NC State. With Duke nine miles away from their arch rival, North Carolina, and twenty minutes away from NC State, Duke fans were waiting for their victory and growing increasingly frustrated.

A group of alums called the Iron Dukes went to the athletic director, Tom Butters. They wanted Coach Mike Krzyzewski gone. "And if you don't get him gone, we're going to get you gone!"

The pressure was enormous for Krzyzewski. His rivals were winning the national championships, were the best in the sport, and people were wondering why Duke wasn't on par with them. Compared to the legend and Mr. Popular who coached the other schools, Mike was a disappointing third wheel. That's tough. His very own people, the Iron Dukes, the people who gave the money, wanted him out.

He had one bad recruiting class, but ultimately, jobs are open for a reason. They weren't winning for a reason. Duke, at one time, was a power in college basketball, but they fell off. Even so, Duke had not won a national championship in their history. The monster of comparison was alive and well. Many times Mike's wife was worried..."How long are we going to be here?"

Having received the letters from the Iron Dukes, what did the athletic director do? He gave the struggling coach a contract extension. Basically, this gesture meant that either Krzyzewski would do well or both Butters and Krzyzewski were going to be fired. Athletic director Tom Butters put everything on the line to show that he supported Krzyzewski. He knew that Krzyzewski was feeling immense pressure to perform, and he asked himself how he could get his coach to relax. "I've got to go all in on my coach, and let him know I've got his back."

Ryan Holiday, who wrote *The Obstacle is the Way*, talks about how what stands in the way becomes the way, and that's really what Krzyzewski did. What was in the way were these great powers. Being so close, their fans were his fans.

For this guy to live in the shadow of two legends and become one himself is very rare, almost impossible. Most people would just quit and say, *You know what? I'll go somewhere else where it's easier,* but Krzyzewski didn't.

Weight lifted off his shoulders with the support of his athletic director, Krzyzewski went out, recruited his tail off, and got a great class of kids. Those kids ended up playing in the Final Four in Dallas in 1986 and then advanced to the national championship. They ended up losing the championship, but that was Krzyzewski's first team that went to the Final Four.

After making it that far, it was known that Duke was a good team. They were competing with NC State and North Carolina.

Somehow, the dude with the funny name ended up going to more final fours. In fact, he ended up winning five final fours in five straight years, making Krzyzewski the winningest division one men's coach of all time.

The craziest thing is he made the Final Four and lost in the 1986 title game to Louisville. Duke came back to the Final Four in 1988, then in 1989, and then in 1990 to lose the national championship by thirty points to UNLV. But then, the very next year they came back and beat the UNLV team that had drilled them by thirty points in the 1991 Final Four as they went on to defeat Kansas to win Duke's first national championship. Then, the Blue Devils went ahead and won the national championship the next year. That's five straight years to the final four. That is unheard of.

We can look back and remember that all fingers were pointed at Krzyzewski, saying he was the problem. He ended up becoming the solution.

It was controversial for Duke to even hire Mike Krzyzewski because he was coaching at Army, and Army was no powerhouse. He wasn't winning a ton of games. Even though he was doing a really great job at a tough job, you would never see a guy like him hired, or last as long as he did, today because we live in a microwave society. Everything has to be instant now. You're not allowed to grow. You have to win right away, right now. You don't get time to make mistakes.

Krzyzewski was allowed to grow and make mistakes, and he ended up becoming a legend. Butters, the athletic director saw Mike's potential, believed in him, and wasn't afraid to give him the time to grow and become the legend he became. You need people in your corner who are going to get there with you and allow you that growth.

The athletic director kept those letters from the Iron Dukes as a reminder of what he went through. He lived through an incredibly tough time, but ultimately those letters are a reminder that despite that rough road, he made the right decision.

Sometimes the standard in the environment around you is so high that, as you strive to meet that high standard, you work so hard that you surpass it. Sometimes the best way to become great is to be around greatness. Sometimes when you're around the great ones, you stumble a bit, but you go on and you do well. Even if the bar is high, guess what. You don't necessarily have to jump over that bar to be a star and be great in your own right. In the right environment, all you need is perseverance.

Mike Krzyzewski was an Army Cadet trained at West Point Military Academy. There's something about people who serve. Soldiers don't back down. My dad was in the Army, and he understood the long-term art of war. Krzyzewski ended up, in basketball terms, going to war with the legend in the ACC conference, Dean Smith. A lot of people didn't survive going up against this guy, ultimately being fired. Mike Krzyzewski survived and thrived! He not only met the bar, he surpassed the bar.

Krzyzewski was an assistant on the first Olympic basketball team, the Dream Team, in 1992 with Michael Jordan, Magic Johnson, Larry Byrd, Charles Barkley. He had been there for what a lot of people think was the team that introduced the world to the game. He understood what it meant to be around rockstar players and what winning meant.

When USA Basketball made Krzyzewski the Olympic team head coach, America had finished with a bronze medal in the 2004 Athens Games, which was, for us, an embarrassment. Basketball is an American made sport, and we dominated it forever. When America didn't win a gold medal in men's basketball, people were shocked and angry. They turned to Krzyzewski needing him to fix USA Basketball. There were top guys who didn't want to play for America. Krzyzewski told them, "You are doing this for your country." To get millionaire athletes to do something nowadays is tough, especially during their off seasons, but this guy went and did it. That's a serious skill. Now, top players are putting their egos aside and playing for the United States. At the 2008 Olympic games, Krzyzewski coached the Redeem Team. They went 8-0 and won the gold medal. Today, Krzyzewski has been the head coach of the USA men's basketball team for the past three Olympics, and they've won the gold medal three times.

To put his career in perspective, he started coaching at Duke in 1980 when Jimmy Carter was president, and he's still coaching to this day, now in his 70s. How many people are still working at the same job they had in 1980?

The same guy they wanted to fire because "he wasn't winning enough" became, arguably, the greatest basketball coach of all time. In 2001, Mike Krzyzewski was inducted into the Basketball Hall of Fame.

As a sportscaster, I leverage Krzyzewski's story often. I've learned that some of the great ones aren't great at first. Some people do come out and set the world on fire, but most people don't sell a million copies their first record. People who are coaching for the first time stumble. I've watched that a lot, and I go back to Krzyzewski and remember that not everyone is going to come out of the gate great.

Years ago, the baseball manager here in Dallas-Fort Worth for the Texas Rangers was getting off to a slow start. A lot of people wanted to get rid of the guy. In my column at the time, I shared my perspective, "Give the guy time to implement what he wants to do. Have a little bit of patience. Some of these great ones take some time." They had planned to fire Ron Washington but postponed it for his birthday. This guy ended up being the winningest manager for the Rangers and took them to the World Series two times. Sometimes we have to press pause on how we judge people who are leaders.

When you are faced with a challenge that's really tough, almost too behemoth, how do you do it? You go to work like Mike Krzyzewski and just keep going. Even as your own people are plotting and planning your demise, you keep going. You go recruit, you go sell, you keep pushing, you keep grinding.

How many people in their own challenges are willing to go through the tough obstacles? Most people don't. It's too easy to make excuses and move on to the next thing that seems easier. For us to win the battle, we have to go through it. We can't sidestep them. If you go through each challenge, you reach the success you want. You win. That is what this guy had to do.

TWEETABLE

Success is not instant—persevere and give leaders, including yourself, the time to develop in an environment surrounded by the best of the best.

Seven-time Emmy-winner Newy Scruggs is the sports director at KXAS-TV (NBC) in Dallas Ft. Worth, Texas. You can catch him weeknights at 6 and 10. Sundays, during the NFL season, Scruggs hosts the Emmy award-winning Big Game Sunday.

Scruggs has been in broadcasting since 1992. Along the way, the stops have included gigs in Florence/Myrtle Beach, South Carolina; Austin, Texas; Cleveland; Los Angeles; and since April 2000, Dallas-Fort Worth.

Twitter: @newyscruggs
Facebook: NewyScruggsSports

CHAPTER 35

I Will Persist Until I Succeed

by John Goolcharan

My life has been defined by many moments of me refusing to give up and instead going against the grain. This has been a philosophy that I have held firm throughout my recent life and business journeys. I'm not saying that my life was extra hard but rather that there is always opportunity to remain strong in the face of opposition and persevere. This is an opportunity for me to share my story and encourage others that may be facing obstacles.

I grew up in a rural village on the island of Trinidad, which for a quick geography lesson is the island that is the southernmost in the Caribbean chain of islands. While growing up there, I was a little different from my friends, as I had a strong affinity for academia and business. I believe that I got this ability from my mother, a teacher. She taught us about being resourceful to find the answers to any question that we had. It is this same resourcefulness and determination that I take with me as I embark on every phase of my life. When I attended secondary school (the equivalent of middle and high school) I always ended up in the science classes. This birthed my love of engineering.

While in secondary school, my father became very ill with heart problems, and it was very hard on my family. All our financial resources were drained in medical bills. At the same time, I started a print and photocopy business in which I served my classmates and teachers with a low-cost alternative for their printing needs. This was a major way in which I earned spending money while at school and was also my first business enterprise, which taught me many invaluable lessons regarding business ownership and its struggles. This got me the reputation of a businessman in school, and I liked that feeling. This is why even though I have a master's degree in engineering, I am still a businessman. However difficult it may be at times, business ownership is something that I would not trade for the world. To this day, it has served me well in many ways, from providing for my family to providing a business visa for me in the United States.

When I completed secondary school, I attended the University of the West Indies while working in an oil company to assist with supporting my family. As an 18-year-old making close to six-figures, this was impressive. But even then, I was not happy. I knew that I had more to offer and to get out of life than working for money in a job that I was unhappy with yet still duty-bound to. This was a turning point in my life as I decided to throw caution to the wind and attend university in the United States to provide a better life for myself and my current and future family. Now, this was not easy. At the age of 18, I was the primary breadwinner of my family, and my family would now be giving up a large portion of income. Still, my mother was very supportive of me, and she did not want me to continue the cycle of everyone around me. Sometimes for cycles to be broken, drastic action needs to be taken. Additionally, we understood that depending on a job was not the way to be truly independent, especially when your job relies on a commodity which moves in drastic cycles such as oil and gas.

While attending university and working, I began attending SAT classes and signed up for the exam to begin my journey to the United States. The night before I was to take the SAT exam, my mother reached out to me via the telephone and said that I needed to go to the hospital immediately. My heart sank. I was terrified of what I would see when I got to the hospital.

Sure enough, my father was connected to tubes and machines that were keeping him alive. He had suffered a massive heart attack and required emergency surgery.

The next day, as I wrote my SAT examination, I prayed for focus, strength, and determination for myself and my family, and for a couple hours I was able to focus on the task at hand and complete my examination. As the famous phrase goes, "Fortune favors the brave." I was successful in my examinations and got accepted at a few universities in the United States.

I chose to attend Florida International University in Miami, FL because of its proximity to the Caribbean and vibrant culture. I needed to get a financial statement that showed that my family could afford to pay all my fees throughout the course of my study. Our family funds were still completely depleted. It took bravery from me and my family to ask my aunt for a sponsor document on which I was able to list her as my financial support for university. This would allow the school to issue my documentation that I needed to deliver to the United States Embassy in Trinidad.

Now, the documentation was sent to me via regular mail. In reality, even though it was being sent internationally, this documentation should have only taken a couple days to process and arrive in Trinidad. However, it seemed as if it were a true test of my ability to keep hope alive and preserve when the documentation did not come in for weeks. It got to the point that school had started, and I would not be able to attend that semester if it took any longer. My heart was racing each day as I searched the mail in the hopes that my documentation would come. I remember August 19, 2010 as clear as day, when the university told me that if the documentation did not arrive by the next day, I would not be able to attend school.

At that moment, my life felt over, yet still there was a fire inside of me burning deeply, aided by the words of my mother beckoning me to continue persevering and moving forward. I remember that evening, visiting and calling each post office in Trinidad asking them to assist with finding my documentation. With each negative answer, I felt myself grow wearier. Yet still, I was determined, as it was my desire to succeed. That evening, my mother recited a verse entitled "I will persist until I succeed," from the book *The Greatest Salesman in the World* by Og Mandino, and at that moment I felt the fire within me continue to burn. Around 9pm, I went home defeated with the only thought in my mind *I will persist until I succeed.*

The next day, my mother called to tell me she received the documentation in the mail. My heart jumped for joy, and I moved on to the next step. I went online to book an appointment at the United States Embassy, and to my shock, I saw that there were no appointments for three months. I decided to book an appointment three months away and take my chances by going to the Embassy in the morning. I got there before the crack of dawn and explained my situation to the guard. Thankfully, they allowed me to have an appointment. At that moment, I knew nothing could stand in my way. After an interview at the Embassy, I received my visa.

The next few days, I said goodbye to my friends and family, and with optimism, I boarded a plane and set off for Miami. I landed there with no idea where I was to live or where the school was located, but within the next few days, I was at university attending classes and set up for success. It was truly after this experience that I felt that my life began. Since then, I have gone on to be a researcher, obtain my master's degree in mechanical engineering, have my research published, start a business, and so many other things. But, I believe that my mentality was shaped by that moment when things became difficult and I refused to lay down. Instead, I became determined to do what needed to be done for success.

It is with this same perseverance that I have started my business to provide syndication and asset management for real estate and business transactions. Since inception in 2016, the goal of my business is to build truly collective wealth for myself, clients, equity partners, and anyone that participates in a deal. The road to find the perfect match of clients, deals, and financing has not been easy, but I have remembered the lessons that I learned and I am persevering to keep proving value in each deal that I enter. A major goal of each transaction that my business enters into is to find deals that can provide cash flow, appreciation, and principal reduction, which translates into building serious wealth and net worth for clients as they share in the ownership benefits of the transactions. Due diligence is taken very seriously, and as a company, we are constantly educating ourselves on every aspect of a deal before closing. As a part of the careful selection process, deals are vetted based on performance from day one and must provide double digit annual returns, which translates into wealth and increased net worth for all involved.

My golf coach told me a phrase that I believe to be true for life and business: "Golf is nothing more than a game of good misses." I must say that if you have a deep desire to do something, be determined to go for it and have the discipline to not let anything get in your way. I want you to be encouraged that just like me, with each step, the fire within you will burn brighter, and you too will know that you can persist until you succeed.

TWEETABLE
Life and business is like golf—nothing more than a game of good misses.

John Goolcharan has been a mechanical engineer and project manager for over $1B in projects. He is also an author and accomplished motivational speaker. He has syndicated, brokered, and managed real estate and businesses in the United States and the Caribbean since 2016. Due to the careful deal selection process, clients have seen on average 10% cash-on-cash returns and 20% ROI through his deals, which builds wealth and net worth for all involved. If you would like to know more about building net worth and wealth, please contact John Goolcharan at info@lasoroc.com or 786-263-8300.

CHAPTER 36

Nothing Can Stop You When You Are Driven and Determined

by Frederick Crawford

I am the eldest of four children born to the late Rev. Dr. Fletcher C. and Mrs. Arnetta Crawford. It was a great feeling being a child of a great pastor. People knew our family because of my dad's reputation. However, it had its drawbacks. My parents had great expectations. As children, we would find ourselves being role models for other children. My parents would tell us how we were to conduct ourselves in the church as well in the community. I grew up thinking I had to be perfect, and that there was no room for shortcomings. My parents also were big on education and its value. My parents talked to my siblings and I often about my nine cousins who were born and raised in New York City housing, also known as "The Project," located in Harlem, NY. My parents were so proud of them since they all went to college and did well.

Here was my dilemma. I could not compete with my cousins or even my younger brother. I had a hard time comprehending in school. I didn't have a behavioral problem or an attention disorder, nor was I consider a "special ed" student. I thought maybe I should have been placed in the special education class. They were at a much slower pace. My brother was a very bright student, and I would watch as he brought home good grades. I would hear my parents praise him, and I wouldn't want to show my report card.

I thought I was unable to excel in school. In the fifth grade, I would sign my homework: Dr. Frederick Crawford. One day during open school night, my teacher, Ms. Scott, showed my mother, who had no idea of my new signature, my homework papers. My mother told the teacher that she would have me change that. But my teacher laughed and said, "Please don't. You never know what may become of him. He might just turn out to be a doctor or someone great." Well, those words stayed with me. Even though I continued to struggle academically, I never forgot Ms. Scott's encouraging words.

In middle school, I was told I would not graduate and would probably have to repeat a grade. One day in class, my teacher said to me in front of the entire class that he didn't see me graduating from junior high school. Well, as it turns out and perhaps against the school policy, the school graduated me.

Upon entering high school, I would hear those words again, "You will not graduate." In my junior year of high school, my brother and I made the varsity basketball team. The coach would get me help with my studies and when it was time for me to apply to colleges, he made calls to help find a scholarship. My coach thought the opportunity would help me to improve my grades. Thank GOD, with of all the help of my tutors, after school programs, and extra-curricular activities I was able to graduate on time.

The scholarship didn't work out because of my grades. My dad was fine with me not receiving a basketball scholarship. He preferred for me not to play basketball so I could focus on college. I applied to a Christian college in Pennsylvania that my mother had heard about. Unfortunately, I was turned down, but they recommended that I attend a junior college for one year then transfer. I found a small Christian junior college in Pennsylvania where I was accepted on probation. My parents were happy to know their child was off to college. My dad would remind me who I was, I was a son of a pastor, and that this was my chance to prove I had the ability to make something of myself. He told me not to try out for the basketball team "no matter what" and to focus.

I was excited and wanted to show my parents I could do it. I was ready to apply myself to school. One day, on my way to class, a couple guys on the basketball team asked if I would like to play during break. I accepted because it was only recreational.

After playing, unbeknownst to me, they went and spoke with the college's basketball coach. Later in the week, the coach watched me play, and he asked me to try out. "You would be an asset to the team," the coach would say. I told him of the conversation my father had with me and that he would not approve of me playing. He asked, "Would it be alright for me to call your dad?"

I was hesitant and nervous, but I told the coach it was up to him. He made the call and was on the phone with dad for quite a while. After talking with my dad, my dad reluctantly agreed to me joining the team as long as I kept my grades up.

The coach was right about me being an asset to the team. That year I was the team's leading scorer, averaging 25 points a game, and second top scorer in the league. I was named rookie of the year and the league most valuable player. Our team was in two conferences, and I made the all-star team as a starter for both conferences.

Unfortunately, my academics suffered, and after one year in college, my GPA was 1.91. I knew I would not be able to transfer to another college. One day, as GOD would have it, four of my friends who were sophomores were applying to other colleges. They decide to go check out a Christian college in Virginia. They invited me to go, and I went just for the ride. If it was a good experience, maybe I could apply the following year because I knew my GPA was too low to transfer at this point.

My friends decided to apply right on the spot. Not to look out of place while they were filling out the application, I went ahead and applied as well. All four of my friends were accepted for the next semester at Eastern Mennonite College and Seminary. I also received a letter, and to my surprise, it was an acceptance letter! Can you imagine how I felt at that moment? I was so happy and surprised to know I would be attending college with my friends. As fate would have it, three of my friends decided not to go, but Stan, my best friend in junior college, decided to attend.

Stan and I would be roommates for the next three years. I didn't try out for the team, and my first year I didn't play on the team. I worked very hard my first year but still didn't get the grades my parents expected and that I desired. My second year, I made up my mind that I was going to work even harder, and as fate would have it, the basketball coach came to the gym while I was playing basketball during a school tournament. About a week later, the basketball coach asked me to join the team. Once again, my dad reluctantly approved.

For the next two years in college, I would find myself on academic probation, and like the high school coach, the college basketball coach provided resources that helped me get through my classes. I had to speak to the president of the university and the counselors every other semester to explain why I should be accepted back into their college.

Yes, I graduated and received a BA degree (bachelor of arts in business administration) from Eastern Mennonite College and Seminary with a 2.12 GPA. It was not the GPA I was working for, but I made it through and proved some of my teachers and critics wrong. There were even individuals in my high school and college who didn't think I would do it. Yes, it was hard for me, but whenever I got discouraged or wanted to drop out of college, I would hear the words in my head, "I knew you couldn't do it," and that motivated me not to give up. I would push myself to work just a little harder. I didn't want to let down my fifth-grade teacher Ms. Scott who allowed me to continue to sign my name Dr. Frederick Crawford.

Happy to graduate with my bachelor's degree in business, I thought once home I would find a job immediately. Needless to say, my thoughts of being hired right away were wrong. Finding a job was difficult, and after looking for a year, I was hired as a bank teller.

Up to this point, outside of Christian books, I had not read a book in its entirety. One day, my dad said, "If a person goes to college and graduates, and no one can tell the difference in their conversation, they ought to go and get their money back." I didn't think dad was talking about me, but it cut me deeply, and became the turning point. I decided that day, I would become a reader and learner.

Around that time my brother introduced me to Amway. He was excited and shared his excitement with me. I joined Amway even though I knew nothing about network marketing. Amway introduced me to the concept of personal development. I learned the books to read, cassette tapes to listen to, and seminars to attend. I discovered that there was so much more to life. I started reading books and listening to personal development tapes three hours a day. I was reading and listening to Napoleon Hill, W. Clement Stone, Dr. Norman Vincent Peale, Earl Nightingale, Zig Ziglar, Jim Rohn, Brian Tracy, Og Mandino, David J. Schwartz, Dale Carnegie, Wallace D. Wattles, and James Allen just to name a few. Soon, my dad would make me his assistant and put me over the youth group. I credit this to personal development.

Besides reading, I started attending personal development seminars. I developed self-confidence in every area of my life. Just a few disciplines done correctly made such a difference. There was such a shift taking place that many spoke of it.

One Friday afternoon, my dad received a call from a church who needed someone to preach for them that coming Sunday. My dad consented for me to go and gave me specific instruction.

That Sunday both services were amazing. That afternoon, the pastor of the second church told the church I was with, "I don't know what you are looking for, but here is your pastor," and pointed directly at me. Speechless and shocked, I felt him plant a seed in my mind. I knew his words were only a compliment, but he also planted a seed in the mind of the people.

The chairman of the deacon board asked if I would come back the following Sunday. I told him after I spoke to my dad, I would give him my answer.

I shared with Dad how the services went and that the church had invited me back. He knew they were not interested in me being their pastor, so he sent me back. He told me what they were looking for in a pastor. Based on what he shared, it was clear I didn't qualify, and that was fine with me. The church was looking for someone who had pastoral experience, in their 40s, and married. Well, I had no experience. I was 24 and not married. My mind was saying one thing to me, but deep down I knew the LORD had a seed growing inside of me.

For the next nine Sundays, I would preach at this church. One Sunday, I was asked to meet with the deacons. On my way to the meeting, Dad and I were talking. Out of nowhere, I heard the LORD say inside of me, "The deacons are going to offer you the pastor's role." And, that's exactly what happened. I became their next pastor.

I knew I needed to continue my personal development routine in order to be a good pastor, I began to read more books on leadership. I also attended leadership seminars. I joined several coaching programs for the purpose of growth.

I knew that my ability to learn and absorb information was paying off in a noticeable way. Besides the many compliments I was receiving, my dad told me how proud he was of me.

One night, I heard the Lord say to me that there were many Christians who were getting caught up in foolishness on Facebook. The Lord told me not to preach against Facebook because it is a helpful tool just misused. He said, "I just want you to post scripture every day and see what I will do." After a month, I noticed many others start posting scriptures as well. Then, I created a group called FaithBook where people could go to escape the negative stuff that was being posted. Around that same time, I was inspired to start a call-in prayer line on Thursdays at 6 a.m. weekly.

While away for the week, I announced that I would be on every morning at 6 a.m. for prayer. When the week was over, I got several calls asking if I would continue every day. I did this prayer line five days a week for over a year.

One morning, I remembered being asked, "How do you stay so calm and always seem to be happy?" I shared with them my daily routine. That gave me an idea. The next day I got on the live call, I shared with my callers what I learned and practiced every morning. I was doing several steps every morning. One day the Lord revealed to me how to break the steps down and get the same results. So, I shortened the process, added one step, and I called it "Commanding Your Mornings." It was the six disciplines I did when awaking first thing in the morning.

The words of my dad, "If a person goes to college and graduates and no one can tell the difference in their conversation, they ought to go and get their money back," changed my life, and I began to push myself to be above average. I now pastor a church of over 500 congregants. I started a church in South Africa in 2018. I am a certified high performance coach, a mentor to ministers, and creator of a coaching program for young pastors and now "Commanding My Life" events.

TWEETABLE

If you want to have a great day it starts with you. How you start your day really does affect the rest of your day!

Pastor Frederick Crawford is the senior pastor of Union Missionary Baptist Church of The Bronx, NY, USA and of Mpumalanga, South Africa. He is a public speaker and certified high-performance coach as well as president of Frederick Crawford Ministries (FCM). FCM offers personal development events and one on one coaching. The Ministry has developed a powerful seminar on "How to Have a Healthy Church" and "Commanding My Life" events.

pastorfcrawford@gmail.com
https://www.facebook.com/fcm.ny/

CHAPTER 37

From Valet Parking for $9 an Hour to a Million Dollar Real Estate Portfolio in 18 Months

by Quentin McNew

H ow much would your focus change after a week long cruise in the Caribbean with Robert Kiyosaki and the biggest names in real estate investing? It was one thing to hear podcasts and read books on these real estate and investing icons, but it was a whole new world being on a week long cruise in our own investing ecosystem. The social interaction with these accomplished investors made me realize how impressive they are as growth-minded people that naturally make you strive to be better, but I also realized that they put their pants on one leg at a time just like me. I didn't quite know it at the time, but that week would be the most memorable education week of my life.

I was just commissioned as Second Lieutenant in the Army National Guard and was finishing up my masters degree at the University of Illinois. I was doing the conventional route of get good grades, go to college, work for 20-30 years, and retire. I started to think about what job would be next as my formal education was coming to an end.

I got the A's and B's and followed the society norms, but I also got caught up in the social life in college. My days were planned around what bar specials to hit up after class on Green Street. The only benefits of hitting the bar as a daily routine were my Chase Sapphire credit card rewards and getting three times points for dining out. I must admit those free flights did come in handy later down the road traveling to seminars. Still, I had to "confront the brutal facts" as Jim Collins said in his book *Good to Great* and get back to the drawing board, since I was going to need a job to pay the bills in the future.

"If you don't find a way to make money while you sleep, you will work until you die."
– Warren Buffett

My desire to create a business came after reading this quote from one of the greatest investors of all time. It made me curious to learn about businesses that provide passive income. I worked valet parking at the Champaign Country Club at $9 an hour plus tips for five years while in college. I didn't stay working there that long because of the pay; instead it was the people I interacted with and the position I had to see the lifestyle that is possible. Besides, driving nice vehicles was a daily dose of motivation, especially for me, when my personal car was a 2008 Honda Civic purchased at a drug seized car auction for $2900. I wanted to have time freedom and knew I needed to build assets and systems that complement that lifestyle.

Not long after I found Warren Buffett's quote, I read that "90% of all millionaires become so through owning real estate," as said by Andrew Carnegie. I knew starting real estate investing wouldn't be about the money, it would be about the freedom it can provide and getting my time back. I would rather fail going for early retirement and chasing that digital nomad lifestyle than accept society's norm to work for 20-30 years. If I failed in real estate investing, then it would be because of my choices and not the asset class of real estate. I had my college education and military background to fall back on if business didn't work out. I figured what's the worst that could happen if I failed? My worst case scenario was most people's everyday life. I could go get a job and do the conventional route. Being in the military part-time, I gained perspective hearing life and death scenarios on missions failing. This made the idea of possibly failing in business a little more acceptable.

I simply couldn't follow the crowd and expect a different result, so I knew it was time to be intentional about building my network and actually start my real estate investing journey with education. I met Dave Zook, a successful syndicator at a syndication event, who gave me a perfect quote for that time in my life: "You can be conventional or you can be wealthy." Dave has raised over 100 million dollars for various investment deals and got me motivated to start syndicating for assets. I got to work implementing systems and processes for real estate investing, then reached out to friends who might be interested in investing in real estate deals that provide returns above what they can get in the stock market. I had the perfect business model leaving that event: "I will leverage our W2 income and credit scores efficiently to start structuring deals for passive income." The first two friends I asked jumped on board. We opened an LLC, and that was the start to an investment business.

My first real estate purchase ended up being a four bedroom, three bath house right next to the University of Illinois for $138,000. I rented two bedrooms to friends for $400 a month and then did Airbnb short-term rental with the third bedroom. The income for the three bedrooms averaged around $1700, and my mortgage was around $920. So, I was profiting a little over $700 a month from one purchase. I was hooked from there and didn't look back.

The real estate business is simple to understand, but it certainly isn't easy. As Mike Tyson says, "Everyone has a plan till they get punched in the mouth." Persistence and having a strong enough "why" are two factors that keep me in the real estate game—even after taking some punches. When managing property, it won't be *if* something breaks, it's *when* something breaks. You will need to go through the bad times and struggles to truly appreciate the good times. Today, I always say you are either getting paid or getting an education in real estate. You only lose when you don't learn from the situation. I count my lessons, not my losses.

Starting the real estate business would require sacrifices, but this was nothing new to me. I knew joining the military out of high school would require saying goodbye to summer night parties with my friends, weddings, and celebrating my birthday at home. I signed up for it and took that calculated risk knowing it would be something proud to look back on.

I always believed in studying and modeling someone who was where I wanted to be. When I played quarterback in high school and college, I always watched Tom Brady and Aaron Rodgers. I wanted to study their footwork, how quick they got the ball out of their hand, and the passion they played with during the game. I took the concept of modeling someone successful over to the real estate arena. I believed in finding someone who had achieved what I wanted, then paying them for the experience, books, and education. If I wasn't willing to invest in myself, then why would anyone else want to?

The first real estate event I attended was a The Real Estate Guys syndication event in Dallas, Texas. The special speaker was lawyer George Ross, who was the advisor for Donald Trump (now President Trump) for over 40 years in Manhattan. I got to learn about the 40 years of experience he had with "The King of Debt," how they negotiated monster deals, structured debt and equity, and managed the cash flow, and I even got to have a couple glasses of red wine after the event with the legend himself. This event was the moment that led me to hearing about all the big names that would be on the Investor Summit at Sea—a week long trip with famous investing icons.

The barrier to entry was high because of the price tag, but that is why I needed to make this event. I had enough experience with free events that end up being sales pitches. I imagined the caliber of people I would meet at an event with an expensive price tag. What made this trip even more special was that the speakers weren't paid to come, they chose to come on their own time. I knew how important my network was to my success and knew this was a once in a lifetime event to build my network. Every time I had growth in my life it was from being surrounded by the right people and leveraging each others strengths efficiently. I always enjoyed being in a team atmosphere and progressing toward shared goals. It didn't matter if that was winning a conference championship in sports or completing a mission in the military.

I soon found out that successful people tend to be lifelong learners with a growth mindset and that they constantly invest in building their network. A top five favorite book of mine is *Mindset* by Carol Dweck. The book holds great stories and data showing how everything is learnable and achievable with a growth mindset. She tells you to stop justifying your inaction with excuses as to why you can't achieve something. Discipline and practice can get us what we want. Some may say, "You can't teach an old dog new tricks." Yes you can, it just takes time. You can cultivate personal development through your efforts, application, and experience. As Henry Ford famously states, "Whether you think you can, or you think you can't, you're right."

I reflected on the past and realized that I wasn't always conscious of who I got advice from. I found out in business that free advice can be the most expensive. I used to ask people who've never been where I wanted to go for directions. Robert Kiyosaki and the famous names on The Real Estate Guys Investor Summit at Sea had been where I wanted to go. Early in one of Robert Kiyosaki's presentations during the event, he said a powerful phrase that will stay with me forever. He said: broke people say, "I can't afford it" and let themselves off the hook. Wealthy people think "How can I afford it?" and put their brain to work. Asking "how" always stimulated my creativity. I believe you don't truly become a real estate investor until you run out of money. Being told I couldn't afford buying my first investment property didn't stop me. I found five zero percent interest credit cards for 12 months. I used those credit cards to buy gold, sold the gold right away to liquidate the gold into cash, then used that cash as a down payment on my first $32,000 house that rented for $640. Later, I would build off that process to buy a property with one credit card, fix it up with another credit card, rent it out, and refinance with my partners to pay off all the credit card debts. I knew one deal wouldn't determine my future, but being resourceful and learning the process would.

Our next session with Robert Kiyosaki was even more powerful. As if reading his books *Rich Dad Poor Dad* or *Cashflow Quadrant* didn't totally change the financial trajectory of my life, the next couple hours in the same room with him would. He spoke about the phrase "be, do, have."

His session related back to a quote by the legendary Jim Rohn: "Your level of success will rarely exceed your level of personal development, because success is something you attract by the person you become." You can't answer the question of "how" someone does something, without asking the question of "who" they became first. I realized that it wasn't what I needed to do, it was who I needed to become. Your outer world only gets better after your inner world does. Jim Rohn says, "Set a goal to become a millionaire for what it will make of you to achieve it." This struck me, and I understood that what you become in the process is more important than the dream itself. Or to put it in other terms, it's not what you get that makes you valuable to the marketplace, it's what you become that makes you valuable to the marketplace. I am constantly listening to audiobooks, podcasts, and reading books because you're either growing or you're dying.

I took with me an idea or quote from every book that I read. The Jim Rohn quote, "Formal education will make you a living; self education will make you a fortune," gave me desire to start a business and never stop learning. The book *The Richest Man in Babylon* taught me to spend less than you earn, to pay yourself first, and to seek wisemen and influenced me to study the most successful real estate investors and model them. The book *The Go Giver* explains the law of value and how your true worth is determined by how much more you give in value than you take in payment. The three biggest things that I have taken away after surrounding myself with all these experiences with some of the biggest names in investing are to constantly focus on your goals, be a lifelong learner reading books, and build your network, because as Jim Rohn says, "You are the average of the five people you spend the most time with."

When you see the track record of someone with massive success, it is easy to get overwhelmed and think that it isn't possible for you. You don't see the failures or the growth they had on their way to the top. I am huge believer in time blocking to the now and reverse engineering from the destination you want. Setting goals and targets will let you know if you are staying on track. In the military during land navigation, we call it azimuth checks. You want to look up and do periodic azimuth checks to verify your progression or readjust, so you don't miss your target. I didn't know that I would end up on this cruise, meeting investors from all over the world that I would later do real estate deals with and still talk to today. You never know how one idea or one relationship can change your life. I stayed active in being a lifelong learner and building my network. I went as far as I could see, and when I got there, I saw further. I have been intentional about putting myself in environments with the best in business and surrounding myself with people that are where I want to go.

When flying, you are told "put the oxygen mask on yourself, before assisting others." I have invested the work on myself and have the proof of concept with results. So, the next step that I am excited about is educating and helping others reach the lifestyle goals they wish to have.

TWEETABLE
Starting real estate investing wouldn't be about the money, it would be about the freedom it can provide.

Quentin McNew is a real estate investor, syndicator, and a First Lieutenant in the Army National Guard. He is the creator of an investment firm McNew Capital LLC that invests in real estate and alternative assets for passive income. He obtained a bachelors and masters degree from the University of Illinois Champaign-Urbana in sports management. He has amassed over 20 rental units totaling over one million dollars in his real estate portfolio in less than 18 months including coffee farmland in Boquete, Panama. His email is mcnewcapital@gmail.com. Contact Quentin if you want to learn more about investment options and real estate investments.

CHAPTER 38

15 Exercises to Build Your Desire, Discipline and Determination

by Robert Helms

Realize what you really want. It stops you from chasing butterflies and puts you to work digging gold."

– William Moulton Marston

S tarting 25 years ago, each new year, I step back from my projects in international real estate development and with The Real Estate Guys™ to bring about The Create Your Future Goals Retreat. What I share with those who attend is my passion, my purpose. Much more than a seminar about setting and achieving compelling goals, it's a hands-on workshop in a carefully created and very focused environment guiding participants to rekindle their most compelling ambitions.

Everything we do that weekend stems from one question: What do you want out of life?

That's a big question, but not a rhetorical one. You've heard it said that you can't hit a target you cannot see. So, how clear is the target you're aiming at?

All of life's achievements begin with desire. At the root of everything you do is a reason that matters. While not always obvious, if you'll drill down to the core of why you do anything, you will discover a desire you have to either accomplish or avoid something. To get the most out of life, you'll need to get clarity on what you really want.

Knowing what you want, however, isn't enough.

You also need the discipline to carry through. The rubber must meet the road. Denis Waitley points out that most people gravitate towards activities that are tension-relieving, not goal-achieving.

Accomplishment through sheer will is certainly possible, but extremely difficult.

To stay at it, you need determination. The going will get tough. You can't let up, or you'll be let down.

So there you have it...desire, discipline, and determination.

Sounds simple, yet it's easier said than done. So, here are some specific steps you can take to become crystal clear about what you want, then build up the discipline to get it done and the determination to see it through.

Desire

The first step is desire. Carl Sandburg noted, "Nothing happens unless first a dream." Here are five quick exercises you can do to get clarity on what you want.

Take Inventory – Before you begin to think about what you want, figure out what you already have. What skills and talents do you currently possess? What are you really good at? What do you enjoy doing? Consider your life experiences so far. In his excellent book *Good to Great*, Jim Collins says you must "confront the brutal facts." Be honest about your shortcomings. You can't be good at everything. What things should you delegate? What challenges do you currently have? Roy Disney said, "When your values are clear to you, making decisions becomes easier." What do you value the most in life?

Consider the Possibilities – Of all the things you could do, which things should you do? What work gives you the greatest feeling of accomplishment? What can you do for hours on end without getting tired or bored? How can you best use your skills and experience in a meaningful way? Feeling listless? Make a list! If you could be, have, or do anything, what would it be? What are you uniquely suited to achieve?

Practice Zero-Based Thinking – Brian Tracy would have you ask yourself: "Knowing what I now know, would I do this again?" Would you make the same career decision? Would you enter into the same relationships? Think through the things you've done in your life and ask yourself how things would change if you had them to do over. What would you do the same? What would you change, and why?

Remove Money from the Equation - Financial success is important, but all too often people who focus on the money miss the bigger picture. Most wealthy people got that way pursuing something that mattered to them. If you concentrate your energy on discovering and cultivating your life's calling, the money will almost certainly follow. Answer this question: "If money were no object, what would you be doing with your life?"

Make a Dent in the World – Success is bigger than you. When you find a cause that you feel strongly about, you will give it your all. What matters to you? In our Mentoring Club consultations, we ask, "If God put you in charge for a day and you could move just one lever in the world, what would it be? And why?" Spend some time thinking through how your life can truly make a difference. Answer this: How specifically will the world be better as a result of the work you do?

Discipline

Now that you know what you really want, you'll need to establish the proper discipline for achievement. Jim Rohn taught: "There are two types of pain you will go through in life, the pain of discipline and the pain of regret. The difference is that discipline weighs ounces while regret weighs tons." Here are five exercises to implement and strengthen discipline.

Consider All of the Costs – Once you know exactly what you want, you have to be prepared to pay the cost. Time you spend achieving your goals is time that cannot be spent elsewhere. What will you have to give up? What cost are you willing to pay? What is too high a cost? There is a cost of taking the necessary action and a cost of not doing so. Determining the cost of not achieving your goals can help instill the discipline necessary to achieve them.

Let Reasons Fuel Your Achievement – When developing discipline, the "why" is more important than the "what." If you are clear about why it is you want what you want, you will get up everyday and work toward your goals. Use those specific reasons as the fuel that drives you to achieve. When you are tempted to ease up, go back to your "why." Do you have a big goal? Great! Why? Answer that question and use the answer to propel yourself forward.

The Power of Habit – John Dryden said, "We first make our habits, and then our habits make us." The good news is that you can develop daily habits and routines (i.e. disciplines) that can push you in the right direction. But be careful. Good habits are difficult to form and easy to live with. Bad habits are easy to form but difficult to live with. Committing to a daily or weekly routine builds discipline. Make a list of habits that will serve you and examine the current habits you have that may not be serving you.

Say No to the Good to Say Yes to the Great – To achieve what matters, you will have to say no to some things you are currently doing. And some of these things may be things you enjoy and profit from. But you can't get to second base without taking your foot off first. What are the good things you'll have to say No to in order to say Yes to the great things you want?

Set Up Personal Accountability – Sometimes we all need help. Having someone else hold you accountable can be a great tool. Committing to going to the gym by yourself is not as powerful as committing to meet someone else there. You are less likely to fail when you make a promise to another person. The best accountability partners are people who are supportive but don't have a vested interest in your results. Who might help hold you accountable, and how?

Determination

With clear goals and a healthy dose of discipline on your side, here are five exercises to build the muscle of determination:

Start Where You Are with What You Have – People often hesitate to make a life change until...fill in the blank. Until...I have more time, or things settle down at work, or I save enough money.... Who you are and what you have is enough. You don't need to make life-altering changes before you start, just get going. Take a step in the right direction. Momentum will be your friend. List three steps you can take immediately.

Build Your Resolve – Everything you do that catapults you towards your goals provides evidence of success. The more steps you take, the more you can take. Be resolute in your commitment and focus on repeatable base hits, rather than swinging for the fences. How can you best build your resolve? How will you keep going when things get difficult? How much will it take to keep you down?

Find Strength in Commitment – A great definition of commitment is: Doing the thing you said you'd do long after the feeling under which you said it has passed. Taking on the world is easy when you're all fired up. Taking the sometimes mundane steps necessary for achievement gets difficult. But commitment is a powerful driver. Make a list of five small commitments you'll make to yourself that will build your determination to reach your goals.

Burn the Bridges – When you eliminate the ability to retreat, you have no choice but to move ahead. Even when things don't go as planned, you can fail forward. Get the lesson. Retool and move on. As long as you keep failure a possibility, you'll hesitate. Do whatever you need to do to stake your claim. Commit to the path and the process. Don't look back. Make sure every step you take moves you in the direction of your desires. How can you burn the bridges in your life?

Never Give Up – Plain and simple, without any wiggle room: Never give up. If you never give up, you'll eventually get there. It might take longer and cost more. But get there you will. Go ahead and think about quitting. Make plans to surrender. Ponder an easier path. Imagine throwing in the towel. Just don't do it. Don't ever quit. Never give up. Ever.

> *"When you get into a tight place and everything goes against you, till it seems as though you could not hang on a minute longer, never give up then, for that is just the place and time that the tide will turn."*

– Harriet Beecher Stowe

In closing, please understand that there is more at stake than just your future. When you fail to live up to your potential, you rob the world of your gifts. When you take the lazy road, not only do you suffer, but so do your family, your friends, your company, your community, and in fact, all of humanity.

So dream a big dream, and inspire us all with its achievement. We're all rooting for you, and you can do it!

TWEETABLE
When you are clear about what you want and committed to doing whatever it takes, there are no limits on what you can achieve.

*Robert Helms is a professional real estate investor with experience in nine states and six countries. As a former top-producing real estate agent, he and his father Bob Helms, the Godfather of Real Estate, ranked in the top 1% of sales in the world's largest real estate organization. Robert's investment and development companies have past and current projects valued at over $800 million. He is the co-author of **Equity Happens – Building Lifelong Wealth with Real Estate** and the host of the nationally syndicated radio show **The Real Estate Guys™**, now in its 22nd year of broadcast. The podcast version of the show is one of the most downloaded podcasts on real estate and is heard in more than 190 countries. Robert's annual Goals Retreat helps people unlock their potential and provides a blueprint for achievement in all areas of life.*

https://realestateguysradio.com, goalsretreat.com

DESIRE DISCIPLINE & DETERMINATION

Lessons From
Bold Thought Leaders

Receive Special Bonuses When Buying
The *Desire, Discipline & Determination* Book

To Receive, send an Email to
gifts@DesireDisciplineDeterminationBook.com